Collins

English

KS2 English

SATs Practice Workbook

Age 7 – 11

Key Stage 2

SATs Practice Workbook

Nick Barber

Contents

Contents

Root Words

 G Grammar　 P Punctuation　 S Spelling

Challenge 1

1 Underline the root word in each of these examples:

a) useless

b) slowly

c) magician

3 marks

Marks............/3

Challenge 2

1 Complete the sentences below by adding one of these roots (in bold) in the spaces.

| ped/pod (foot) | ject (throw) | hydr (water) | therm (heat) | dict (say) |

a) Firemen can get water from a _____ant in the street.

b) If you press the button on the CD tray, it will e_____ the disk.

c) The teacher _____ated the notes by reading them aloud while the class wrote them down.

d) A _____icure is a beauty treatment for someone's feet.

e) Doctors and nurses often use a _____ometer to take someone's temperature.

f) The photographer used a tri_____ to keep his camera steady.

g) The fortune teller said she could pre_____ what would happen in the future.

h) The dress was in the re_____ sale, but it looked perfect.

i) The _____ostat on the central heating was broken.

j) You need to drink water to stay _____ated.

10 marks

Marks........../10

4

Root Words

Challenge 3

1 Write down the full meaning of these words, based on the clues about the root words. The first example has been done for you. You can use a dictionary to help you.

> Mono = one
> **Monotone** = *one colour*

a) Phobia = fear of something
   Arachnophobia = _____

b) Tele = far
   Telepathic = _____

c) Graph = write
   Autograph = _____

d) Nov = New
   Novice = _____

e) Geo = earth
   Geography = _____

5 marks

GPS 2 Use each <u>full</u> word from question 1 in a sentence to show its meaning.

a) _____
   _____

b) _____
   _____

c) _____
   _____

d) _____
   _____

e) _____
   _____

5 marks

Marks.........../10

Total marks ..../23   How am I doing?

5

Prefixes

G Grammar   P Punctuation   S Spelling

Challenge 1

1 Underline the prefixes in these words.

a) international

b) redecorate

c) unnecessary

d) irregular

e) preview

f) disappear

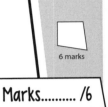

6 marks

Marks.......... /6

Challenge 2

1 Use prefixes to make the opposites of these words.

a) believable   _____

b) healthy   _____

c) agree   _____

d) honest   _____

e) understand   _____

f) fold   _____

g) connect   _____

h) tidy   _____

i) pleasant   _____

9 marks

GS **2** Use the words that you have created in question 1 to complete these sentences.

a) When you have an opposite opinion, you _____.

b) If you pull things apart, you might _____ them.

c) If you do not tell the truth, you are _____.

d) If something is not nice, it is _____.

e) You might _____ a piece of paper.

f) The boys' room was very _____ because they tipped everything on the floor.

g) If something is not clear, you might _____ it.

h) If you don't eat a balanced diet, you might become

_____ .

i) Some people think the existence of aliens is

_____ .

9 marks

Marks......... /18

Challenge 3

1 Circle the word with a prefix that makes sense in these sentences.

a) The architect **redesigned / misdesigned / ildesigned** the house because he got it wrong first time.

b) The television channel broadcasts many **extranational / international / supernational** channels.

c) The keyboard was **re-entangled / unentangled / disentangled** from the messy wires near the computer.

d) The mayor **reveiled / deveiled / unveiled** a statue.

e) People who cannot read or write are **unliterate / illiterate / misliterate**.

f) In some countries it is **unpolite / impolite / dispolite** to wipe your nose in public.

g) Food that has gone mouldy is **inedible / unedible / disedible**.

h) If an idea is shown to be wrong, we can say we **misproved / disproved / reproved** it.

i) Stealing is **mishonest / unhonest / dishonest**.

j) He was expelled from school for **disbehaving / non-behaving / misbehaving**.

10 marks

Marks......... /10

Total marks .... /34   How am I doing?

7

Suffixes

G) Grammar   P) Punctuation   S) Spelling

Challenge 1

1 Underline the suffix in each of these words.

a) hesitantly   **d)** reader

b) wishing   **e)** excitement

c) blockage   **f)** closeness

6 marks

Marks.......... /6

Challenge 2

1 Complete the sentences below by adding a suffix to the underlined word.

(You might need to change the ending of the underlined word before adding the suffix.)

a) The disease was <u>prevent</u> _____ by giving people vaccinations.

b) There was a <u>block</u> _____ in the sink and the kitchen flooded.

c) It was quite <u>nature</u> _____ for girls to play football at the school.

d) The man from Rome was an <u>Italy</u> _____.

e) The scientist specialised in studying <u>molecule</u> _____ biology.

f) The King ruled over his <u>king</u> _____.

g) The boy <u>laugh</u> _____ at the joke.

h) It was the <u>hot</u> _____ day of the year.

i) There were no sports facilities in the <u>neighbour</u> _____.

j) After they won the competition they had a huge <u>celebrate</u> _____.

10 marks

Marks..... /10

Suffixes

Challenge 3

1 Circle the word with a suffix that makes sense in these sentences.

a) The **governade / governed / government** met after the election.

b) They **normaler / normally / normalled** had chips on Friday.

c) There was a great **improvement / improvation / improver** in Josh's spelling.

d) The large print book was very **reading / readed / readable**.

e) Their new bedroom was so **spacing / spacious / spacatious** that they could put two beds in it.

f) After the explanation, the boys were still **clued / cluely / clueless** about what to do.

g) The **motorised / motorated / motorish** model boat sped across the lake.

h) The fence had broken and the broken posts were **dangering / dangered / dangerous**.

8 marks

GS 2 Add a suffix to each noun to make an adjective. The first one has been done for you.

a) accident $\implies$ *accidental*

b) region $\implies$ _____

c) custom $\implies$ _____

d) wonder $\implies$ _____

e) base $\implies$ _____

f) magic $\implies$ _____

g) fool $\implies$ _____

6 marks

Marks......... /14

Total marks .... /30   How am I doing?

Structure and Organisation

Challenge 1

1   Underline the structural feature in each of these lists.

a) **Paragraph / Alliteration / Onomatopoeia**

b) **Plosives / Fricatives / Conclusion**

c) **Introduction / Adjectives / Assonance**

3 marks

Marks.......... /3

Challenge 2

1   Circle the most appropriate joining words to make the passage make sense.

The cousins wanted to go to the football match, **(a) but / and / therefore** their parents didn't. As a result, the day ended up being quite stressful. Amy **(b) and / but / therefore** Anna sulked in the kitchen, **(c) during / since / while** the adults chatted in the living room. **(d) During / After a while / On the other hand**, the girls decided to sneak out and watch the game at their friend's house. Their friend, Belinda, lived at the other end of the street, **(e) afterwards / whenever / although** she didn't normally like football.

They knocked on Belinda's door **(f) which / but / usually** she wasn't in. This was a blow to the girls, but they didn't give up. Their friend Yasmin lived a few houses further down **(g) and / whenever / instead of** they knew that she would be watching the game. **(h) But / Notably / So**, off they trotted and knocked on Yasmin's door. They waited a few moments and sure enough, the door opened, **(i) despite this / but / and** it wasn't Yasmin, it was her mother.

Hi girls – I'm sorry, but Yasmin's poorly with chicken pox. **(j) Whenever / Despite this / Equally**, she's still watching the match in bed. What a shame you can't see her!

10 marks

Marks......... /10

Structure and Organisation

Challenge 3

GPS **1**   On a separate piece of paper, write three paragraphs about an adventure or event. Include the following features in each paragraph to show the purpose and structure of your writing.

Paragraph 1 – introduction

- A short sentence to grab attention.
- Three adjectives to set the scene.
- A rhetorical question to make the reader think.

1 mark
3 marks
1 mark

Paragraph 2 – development

- Two multi-clause (complex) sentences to add extra detail.
- Two personal opinions to help the reader understand your ideas.

2 marks
2 marks

Paragraph 3 – conclusion

- Ellipsis to create a cliffhanger at the end of the paragraph.

1 mark

Marks.........../10

Total marks .... /23   How am I doing?

Using Dictionaries

Challenge 1

1 Put the words in each of these lists into alphabetical order.

a) amazing army armadillo

_____

b) beautiful boat bass

_____

c) cricket crime card

_____

d) tree track tractor

_____

e) lemon limerick laughing

_____

5 marks

Marks.......... /5

Challenge 2

1 Use a dictionary to answer these questions.

a) What does the word *somnambulate* mean?

_____

b) Does *stationery* or *stationary* mean 'to stand still'?

_____

c) Is *antidisestablishmentarianism* a real word?

_____

d) Which language does the word 'frottoir' (a kind of musical instrument) come from? _____

e) What does *achromatic* mean?

_____

f) What does the prefix 'neo' mean?

_____

g) How many people take part in a duet? _____

7 marks

Marks.......... /7

Using Dictionaries

Challenge 3

1   Using a dictionary, find a word that begins with the stated letter and matches the definition.

Word begins with….	Definition
B_____	A bunch of flowers, especially a large, carefully arranged, one.
C_____	Something that helps to solve a problem or unravel a mystery.
D_____	Something that is owed, such as money, goods, or services.
E_____	Something laid by a bird, e.g. a hen.
I_____	A dome-shaped house, usually built from blocks of solid snow.
J_____	A precious or semiprecious stone.
K_____	A light frame covered with a thin material, flown in the wind at the end of a length of string.
M_____	A large, extinct, hairy, elephant-like creature.
N_____	The period of darkness between sunset and sunrise.
O_____	A type of citrus fruit.

10 marks

Marks.........../10

Total marks .... /22

How am I doing?

Prose Genres

G Grammar   P Punctuation   S Spelling

Challenge 1

1 In each list, circle the option that is **not** a type of prose.

a) limerick / essay / biography

b) novel / short story / sonnet

c) e-mail / poem / autobiography

3 marks

Marks.......... /3

Challenge 2

1 Read these extracts. Match the extracts to the prose genres listed below.

Science fiction   Romance   Autobiography   Fantasy   Non-fiction

a) Their eyes met across a crowded room and everything else melted in the sunset. Their hearts pounded as they looked at each other.

_____

b) Bardock the wizard pointed his mighty spear at the thunder clouds releasing a bolt of energy which unleashed four dragons, breathing fire, towards the crumbling castle.

_____

c) I was born in Stoke-on-Trent in 1961, to a working-class family, who descended from a long line of church wardens. We had – and still have, in our family – a biblical dictionary (called a 'Concordance') which has been written in, tracing our family line from the English civil war.

_____

d) The first evidence of settlers in North America was found in prehistoric cave paintings and simple tools. This archaeological evidence leads us to believe that there were settlers in North America at the same time as the pyramids were built in Egypt.

_____

e) Sergeant Smith of the Space Corps strapped on his oxygen pack and stepped into the gleaming space pod, which was to take him to the starship stationed in orbit around Mars.

_____

5 marks

Marks.......... /5

Prose Genres

Challenge 3

GPS 1   Write a paragraph in each of the following prose genres, using the features indicated.

a) Write a paragraph of science fiction, including: space travel, rocket ships and futuristic technology.

_____

_____

_____

_____

_____

_____

3 marks

b) Write a paragraph from an adventure story, including: a car chase, a hero and a villain, and an explosion.

_____

_____

_____

_____

_____

_____

3 marks

c) Write a paragraph from a mystery story, including: a creepy setting, events set at night and a cliffhanger ending.

_____

_____

_____

_____

_____

_____

3 marks

Marks.........../9

Total marks .... /17   How am I doing?

Themes and Conventions

Challenge 1

1 State whether each of these sentences is **true** or **false**.

   a) The theme of a piece of writing is not necessarily the same as the subject. _____

   b) Writing can only have one main theme. _____

   c) Writing can have several minor themes. _____

3 marks

Marks.........../3

Challenge 2

1 Draw lines between the boxes to match each writing type with its typical features (conventions).

Crime fiction	Handsome prince. Beautiful princess. Villain. Magic.
Cowboy stories	Silliness. Exaggeration. Humour.
Comedy writing	Police officer. Criminal. Element of mystery.
Fairy story	Real-life experiences. Personal thoughts and feelings. Often chronological.
Autobiography	Horses. Wild West. Deserts. Ghost towns.

5 marks

Marks.........../5

Challenge 3

1 Read the extract on page 17 from the novel 'Dracula' by Bram Stoker. This is an example of gothic fiction, which often has these conventions:

   a) Bad weather   **d)** Darkness

   b) Sense of mystery and fear   **e)** The power of nature

   c) The supernatural

Themes and Conventions

All of these five features appear in this passage. Underline one example of each.

As the evening fell it began to get very cold, and the growing twilight seemed to merge into one dark mistiness the gloom of the trees, oak, beech, and pine, though in the valleys which ran deep between the spurs of the hills, as we ascended through the Pass, the dark firs stood out here and there against the background of late-lying snow. Sometimes, as the road was cut through the pine woods that seemed in the darkness to be closing down upon us, great masses of greyness, which here and there bestrewed the trees, produced a peculiarly weird and solemn effect, which carried on the thoughts and grim fancies engendered earlier in the evening, when the falling sunset threw into strange relief the ghost-like clouds which amongst the Carpathians seem to wind ceaselessly through the valleys. Sometimes the hills were so steep that, despite our driver's haste, the horses could only go slowly. I wished to get down and walk up them, as we do at home, but the driver would not hear of it. 'No, no,' he said; 'you must not walk here; the dogs are too fierce'; and then he added, with what he evidently meant for grim pleasantry—for he looked round to catch the approving smile of the rest—'and you may have enough of such matters before you go to sleep.' The only stop he would make was a moment's pause to light his lamps.

When it grew dark there seemed to be some excitement amongst the passengers, and they kept speaking to him, one after the other, as though urging him to further speed. He lashed the horses unmercifully with his long whip, and with wild cries of encouragement urged them on to further exertions. Then through the darkness I could see a sort of patch of grey light ahead of us, as though there were a cleft in the hills. The excitement of the passengers grew greater; the crazy coach rocked on its great leather springs, and swayed like a boat tossed on a stormy sea. I had to hold on.

5 marks

Marks.........../5

Total marks .... /13

How am I doing?

17

Picking Out and Commenting on Details

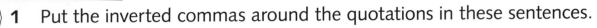

G) Grammar   P) Punctuation   S) Spelling

Challenge 1

P) **1** Put the inverted commas around the quotations in these sentences.

a) The word anxious creates the feeling that the main character is uncertain about what he wants to do.

b) The phrase Don't do it, Freddy! creates the impression that the speaker is angry.

c) By using the adjective clever the writer makes the reader feel sympathy for the main character.

3 marks

Marks............/3

Challenge 2

1 Read the poem below and then answer the questions that follow:

TWENTY LITTLE SNOWFLAKES by Leroy F. Jackson
Twenty little snowflakes climbing up a wire.
'Now, listen,' said their mother, 'don't you climb up any higher.
The sun will surely catch you, and scorch you with his fire.'
But the naughty little snowflakes didn't mind a word she said,
Each tried to clamber faster than his fellow just ahead;
They thought that they'd be back in time enough to go to bed.
But they found out that their mother wasn't quite the dunce they thought her,
The sun bobbed up—remember this, my little son and daughter—
And turned those twenty snowflakes into twenty drops of water.

a) Which word or phrase suggests that the snowflakes will be burnt?

_____

1 mark

b) Which word suggests that the snowflakes are disobeying their mother. _____

1 mark

c) Which word means 'to climb'? _____

1 mark

Picking Out and Commenting on Details

d) 'But they found out that their mother wasn't quite the dunce they thought her' – what does this suggest about the advice their mother gave?

_____

_____

2 marks

Marks.......... /5

Challenge 3

1 The poem in Challenge 2 gives the idea that we should listen to the advice of others. Explain, using the 'Point – Quotation – Comment' system, how this idea is put across. Include two 'Point – Quotation – Comment' examples in your answer.

Point 1 – The first way that the writer suggests that we should listen to the advice of others is seen when… _____

_____

Quotation 1 _____

_____

Comment 1 _____

_____

_____

_____

Point 2 – The second way that the writer suggests that we should listen to the advice of others is seen when… _____

_____

Quotation 2 _____

_____

Comment 2 _____

_____

_____

6 marks

Marks.......... /6

Total marks .... /14   How am I doing?

Types of Poetry

Challenge 1

1 How many lines does a limerick have?

_____

2 How many lines does a sonnet have?

_____

3 How many lines are in a rhyming couplet?

_____

1 mark

1 mark

1 mark

Marks........../3

Challenge 2

1 Draw lines to match the poem types with their correct descriptions.

Poem type

Description

Acrostic

Epigram

Shape poem

Haiku

Ballad

Originally a Japanese poem made of three lines and 17 syllables.

A poem that tells a story.

A poem where the first, last or other letters in a line spell out a word or phrase.

A brief and memorable poem, designed to put over a key idea, often in a funny way.

Usually describes an object – and is shaped the same as the object that is being described.

5 marks

Marks........../5

Types of Poetry

Challenge 3

1   What is the rhyme pattern of a limerick?

_____

1 mark

2   Which topic are sonnets often written about?

_____

1 mark

3   How many lines are there in a quatrain? _____

1 mark

4   In an ABAB rhyme scheme, which lines rhyme?

_____

1 mark

5   What pattern does free verse have?

_____

1 mark

6   How many syllables are there in the first line of a Haiku poem?
Tick the correct answer.

3 ☐   4 ☐   5 ☐   6 ☐

7   Three quatrains and a rhyming couplet would make up what kind
of poem?

_____

1 mark

8   What is special about an acrostic?

_____

_____

1 mark

9   What is the rhyme pattern
of this verse?

_____

Anna ate her eggs and beans.

She munched them down

Without a frown,

But spilled them on her jeans.

1 mark

Marks.........../9

Total marks .... /17   How am I doing?

21

Retrieving Information

Challenge 1

1 State whether each of these sentences is **true** or **false**.

   a) If something is inferred from a text, it is suggested. _____

   b) Less obvious points are picked from a text by reading between the lines. _____

   c) Clearly stated facts can only be picked out by reading between the lines. _____

3 marks

Marks.........../3

Challenge 2

1 Read the short conversations and answer the questions that follow.

   a) A: Look at the big queue! Do you think we'll get in?

   B: I think so. Some of these people already have tickets.

   A: How much are the tickets?

   B: Only five pounds for the first screening. I'll pay.

   A: Thanks. I'll buy the sweets and popcorn.

   i) Where are these people? _____

   ii) What are they talking about? _____

   _____

   iii) Do these people already know each other? _____

3 marks

   b) A: When did this happen?

   B: This morning. I was playing football and I fell over.

   A: Can you walk on it?

   B: No. It hurts a lot.

   A: I think we'll have to take you for an X-ray.

   B: Will I be able to play in the game tomorrow?

   A: I'm afraid not.

Retrieving Information

i)   Where are these people? _____

ii)   Who are they? _____

iii) What are the people talking about? _____

_____

3 marks

Marks.......... /6

1   Read the passage below. Put a tick next to the statements below if they are a valid idea worked out from the passage; put a cross by them if they are not.

> A legend is a popular type of folk tale. In some ways, legends are like myths, another type of folk tale. But myths describe events from way back in time and usually deal with religious subjects, such as the birth of a god. Legends usually tell of actual people, places and events and often take place in comparatively recent times. Some legends are based on real persons or events, but many are entirely fictional. The unbelievable legends of the accomplishments of Robin Hood and King Arthur are thought to be based on real people, but the legends of Napoleon and Josephine are exaggerations of what really happened. Most societies have legends – in Stoke-on-Trent, the witch Mollie Leigh is well-known and she has achieved national fame too.

a)   Both legends and myths can be classified as folk tales. ☐

b)   Myths generally take place in comparatively recent times. ☐

c)   The stories of Robin Hood and King Arthur are probably not true, but they are based on actual people. ☐

d)   Legends about Napoleon and Josephine are not entirely fictional. ☐

e)   Mollie Leigh is only known in Stoke-on-Trent. ☐

5 marks

Marks.......... /5

Total marks .... /14   How am I doing?

Fact and Opinion

 G Grammar   **P** Punctuation   **S** Spelling

Challenge 1

1 State whether each of these sentences is **fact** or **opinion**.

a) One plus one equals two. _____

b) One plus one is a really simple sum. _____

c) One plus one is an addition sum. _____

d) One plus one equals one less than three. _____

e) Everyone knows the answer to one plus one. _____

5 marks

Marks.......... /5

Challenge 2

1 State whether each of these sentences is **fact** or **opinion**.

a) The coat was red. _____

b) The man had lost his car. _____

c) Port Vale is the best football club in the country. _____

d) It's not a very good website. _____

e) You will get cold if you forget your gloves. _____

f) He can win if he trains properly. _____

g) I am the best tennis player. _____

h) I am the world number 1 tennis player at this moment in time, according to the rankings. _____

i) We think Belinda stole the car. _____

j) I didn't have a coat. _____

k) The supermarket is the biggest building in the town. _____

l) The boy band's album was well-liked. _____

12 marks

Marks......... /12

Fact and Opinion

Challenge 3

GPS **1** Write two paragraphs about yourself in which you include five facts and five opinions.

_____

_____

_____

_____

_____

_____

_____

_____

_____

_____

_____

_____

_____

_____

_____

_____

_____

_____

_____

_____

_____

10 marks

Marks......... /10

Total marks .... /27

How am I doing?

Comparing Texts

Challenge 1

1 State whether each of these sentences is **true** or **false**.

a) The form of texts is usually to do with whether they are prose, poetry or drama. _____

b) The structure of texts might be affected by their paragraph lengths. _____

c) The language of texts should never be compared. _____

3 marks

Marks.......... /3

Challenge 2

1 a) Look closely at these two texts. Find and circle the five differences between them.

> **1** Famous female country music singers were often well-known in the 1980s for wearing big wigs and cowboy boots. They might have come from Nashville, Tennessee or Austin, Texas, in the United States. Because of their extreme appearance, they were seen as objects of fun outside North America, but in their own country they were seen as the height of fashion.

> **2** Famous country music singers were often well-known in the 1980s for wearing big wigs and cowboy boots; they might have come from Nashville, Tennessee or Austin, Texas, in the United States. Because of their unusual appearance, they were seen as objects of fun outside America, but in their own country they were seen as the height of style.

5 marks

b) The writer chose text 1 as the final version because he thought it was more precise. Give one reason why he might have thought this.

_____

_____

_____

1 mark

Marks.......... /6

Comparing Texts

Challenge 3

1 Read these two texts and then answer the questions.

> **Text 1**
> According to Greek myths, Deucalion was the righteous son of Prometheus; ancient sources name his mother as Clymene, Hesione, or Pronoia. The anger of the chief god, Zeus was sparked by Lycaon, the king of Arcadia who had done some terrible things. Zeus unleashed a storm so that the rivers ran in torrents and the sea flooded everywhere. Deucalion, with the aid of his father Prometheus, was saved from this flood by building a chest.

> **Text 2**
> According to the Genesis flood story in the Christian bible, God decides to flood the earth because of the sinful nature of mankind. Noah, because he is viewed as a good man, is given instructions to build a big boat called an ark. When the ark is completed, Noah, his family, and two of each type of animals of the earth are asked to enter the ark. When the flood begins, all life outside of the ark perishes. After the waters disappear, all those aboard the ark get off.

a) In both texts, how is the reason for the flood similar?

_____

1 mark

b) In both texts, how is the reason for the flood different?

_____

_____

1 mark

c) Name one similarity between Noah and Deucalion.

_____

1 mark

d) What is the difference between the vessels in which Noah and Deucalion were saved?

_____

1 mark

Marks.......... /4

Total marks .... /13   How am I doing?

27

G Grammar P Punctuation S Spelling

1 Split these words into their prefix, suffix and root word.

Word	Prefix	Suffix	Root Word
a) Unhappiness			
b) Forewarning			
c) Rejigged			

9 marks

2 State whether each of these sentences is **true** or **false**.

a) A paragraph may contain only one sentence. _____

b) 'Aardvark' comes before 'Abacus' in the dictionary. _____

c) A sonnet is a kind of novel. _____

3 marks

GS **3** The underlined words in these sentences have something wrong with their prefix or suffix. Write their correct form so that the sentences make sense.

a) The youth club was a new <u>establishness</u> in the town.

_____

b) The number of people taking part in the project <u>miscreased</u> because they didn't like it. _____

c) The fog <u>misappeared</u> and the sun came out. _____

d) 'That's <u>unpossible</u>!' said the surprised boy. _____

e) The girls did <u>super-curricular</u> activities after school.

_____

f) The demolition machine <u>destroying</u> the wall yesterday.

_____

g) A <u>monopod</u> is a camera stand with three legs. _____

h) A <u>tablic</u> newspaper is different from a broadsheet newspaper because it is smaller. _____

i) The children were in a state of <u>confusedness</u> as they didn't know what to do. _____

9 marks

4 Read this passage and answer the questions that follow.

Formed in the dim and distant past of 1993, in the North of England, Elvis Fontenot and the Sugar Bees have evolved through many line-up changes to become the premier European swamp'n'roll outfit that they are today.

The line-up of Nick Barber (Accordion/Vocals/Frottoir/Mandolin), Paul Asher (Accordion/Fiddle/Mandolin/Bass), Craig Beverley (Lead Guitar/ Vocals), Stuart Duthie (Bass/Harmonica/Vocals) and Chris Plimbley (Drums) returned to play in Louisiana and Texas in 2007, after previously playing at the French Quarter Festival in New Orleans in 2003 and 2005.

In 2006 and 2009, they were crowned 'European Zydeco band of the Year' and Nick won European Rub-board player of the year – they have played the Kilkenny Rhythm and Roots Festival in Ireland on an unprecedented five occasions and have played all over France, Germany, Ireland and Holland as well as the UK. They've also been played on the BBC by Andy Kershaw and Mike Harding and have been on TV in Austin, Texas and featured on radio stations across America and also in Australia.

a) Write down one fact about Elvis Fontenot and the Sugar Bees from the first paragraph.

_____

_____

1 mark

b) Write down one opinion about Elvis Fontenot and the Sugar Bees from the first paragraph.

_____

_____

1 mark

c) The second paragraph implies that the band are versatile musicians. Is this **true** or **false**?

_____

1 mark

d) Give a reason for your answer to part **c)**.

_____

1 mark

e) Compare the second and third paragraphs. What do they both imply about how widely known the band are?

_____

_____

1 mark

5 Read the poem below and answer the questions that follow.

> Dan was a quiet and simple lad
> He'd never had a penny
> For this, however, he was extremely glad.
> He was happier than many.
> Until one day his heart did jump
> He saw his heart's desire
> His blood did start to suddenly bump
> He flew higher and higher.
> Despite his lack of a sparkling penny
> He chased his romantic dream
> Mocked at times by – how many?
> His smiling face did beam
> For Dan knew he had more than gold
> He had a love that would never grow old.

a) What kind of poem is this? _____

1 mark

b) Give two reasons explaining how you worked out the answer to part **a)**.

_____

_____

2 marks

_____

1 mark

c) Who is the subject of this poem? _____

d) What is one of the main themes of this poem? _____

1 mark

e) Underline the rhyming couplet in this poem.

f) How many quatrains are there in this poem? _____

1 mark

1 mark

GS **6** This passage is written in the past tense. Write the missing suffixes to the verbs in the space provided. Change the spelling of the root word ending if you need to.

The boy was run_____ to the shop but soon got out of breath. He snatch_____ some money from his pocket and dash_____ into the newsagent's. He was look_____ for his favourite football magazine but couldn't find it. He went to the counter and ask_____ the shopkeeper if it had come in yet. The shopkeeper reply_____ that it wasn't due in until the weekend. The boy was disappoint_____ but realise_____ that he could now spend the money on something else. He saw that his favourite sweets were on a shelf behind the shopkeeper, so he query_____ how much they were. They were within his price range, so he purchase_____ some.

10 marks

7 In this passage, there are a number of root words, but they are missing their prefix or suffix. Add an appropriate prefix or suffix to make the passage make sense.

The girl was _____raged by the decision to ban selling her favourite sweets from the supermarket because they contained a rare chemical which caused medic_____ problems to some people. She thought that they should still be sold, but with a warning on the pack_____. That way, she argue_____, everybody would be happy. This _____dicted official government advice however, so the girl was not in luck.

5 marks

Marks........ /48

Homophones

Challenge 1

1   Circle the correct word in each sentence.

a)   **There / Their** is the train!

b)   '**Your / You're** not going out dressed like that!'

c)   **It's / Its** impossible.

d)   The music is **to / too / two** loud!

e)   I don't **know / no** if Jay is coming with us.

f)   **They're / Their** going home tomorrow.

6 marks

Marks .... /6

Challenge 2

1   Circle the correct word in each sentence.

a)   She got soaked in the rain, so she had to **ring / wring** out her clothes.

b)   The man's head was completely **bawled / bald**.

c)   On their trip to Turkey, the tourists visited a **bizarre / bazaar**.

d)   They spent a relaxing time on the **beech / beach**.

e)   'Don't pick that **bury / berry** – it's poisonous!'

f)   The **bread / bred** tasted delicious.

g)   They decided to join the long **queue / cue**.

h)   Richard had a **horde / hoard** of empty bottles in his flat.

i)   The priest led the funeral **write / rite / right / wright**.

j)   An **arc / ark** is a giant boat.

10 marks

Marks .... /10

Homophones

Challenge 3

GS **1** Read this passage. The underlined words are homophones, but have they been used correctly?

Complete the table, with the correct answers.

> Caroline wanted to <u>by</u> some new clothes. She knew that she shouldn't, <u>butt</u> she had a job interview coming up and wanted to look her best. Luckily she had been on a sewing <u>course</u> a few weeks earlier and <u>new</u> how to make her own clothes from scratch. She decided to <u>practice</u> her skills by making a <u>pear</u> of trousers first. She <u>rapped</u> the material around her <u>waste</u> to <u>sea</u> if it was long enough and fortunately, it was; <u>whether</u> the trousers would end up being any good, remained to be <u>seen</u>.

Word	Correct? (Yes or No)	If incorrect, how should it be spelled?
by		
butt		
course		
new		
practice		
pear		
rapped		
waste		
sea		
whether		
seen		

11 marks

Marks.......... /11

Total marks .... /27   How am I doing?

Common Misspellings

G Grammar   P Punctuation   S Spelling

Challenge 1

1   State whether each of these words is spelled correctly by placing a tick or a cross in the box.

a) acheived ☐   d) knowlege ☐

b) agressive ☐   e) previous ☐

c) appearance ☐   f) charactors ☐

6 marks

Marks.......... /6

Challenge 2

1   Read the sentences below. Put a tick or a cross in each box to show whether the underlined word is spelled correctly or not. Half of them are correct; half are incorrect.

a) The assasination of President Kennedy happened in the early 1960s. ☐

b) Basically, you should read the instructions. ☐

c) The invention of the seed drill marked the beginning of the agricultural revolution. ☐

d) I beleive in aliens. ☐

e) It is nobody's buisness but mine. ☐

f) The committee decided that the rules were fair. ☐

g) Judie was embarrased by the reaction to her singing. ☐

h) The man was forty years old. ☐

i) His daughter was fourteen years old. ☐

j) The last answer was definately right. ☐

10 marks

S 2   Write the correct spellings of the five incorrectly spelled words in question 1.

_____   _____

_____   _____

_____

5 marks

Marks......... /15

Common Misspellings

Challenge 3

S 1 Read the passage below. All of the underlined words are incorrectly spelled. Re-write the passage, with the words correctly spelled.

> The <u>politican</u> announced in his speech that there were going to be many changes. He <u>refered</u> to the mistakes made by the previous <u>govenment</u> and asked the audience to <u>rember</u> what a mess they had made of the country. He said that these new rules were <u>seperate</u> from what the Prime Minister was going to announce later. He <u>hopped</u> that they would be <u>succesful</u> in bringing back good times to the nation. The audience <u>where</u> surprised by his <u>bowled</u> statements, but many decided to <u>weight</u> until they heard what the Prime Minister would say before making a judgement.

_____

_____

_____

_____

_____

_____

_____

_____

_____

_____

_____

10 marks

Marks......... /10

Total marks .... /31　　　　How am I doing?

Apostrophes

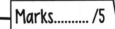 **G** Grammar   **P** Punctuation   **S** Spelling

Challenge 1

GP **1** Read the statements below and decide whether each phrase refers to **one** or **more than one**.

a) The girl's books. _____

b) The girls' books. _____

c) The boys' game. _____

d) The cat's bed. _____

e) The animals' food. _____

5 marks

Marks.......... /5

Challenge 2

GP **1** Put the missing apostrophe in each of these sentences.

a) Brendans taste in music was fantastic.

b) Several people commented on how smart Declans shirts were.

c) Kens video camera was the latest model.

d) Willies record shop was the friendliest in Ireland.

e) Chriss post on the internet forum was liked by lots of people.

f) Dunkys name was very strange, but it was a real name.

g) No one understood Lauras handwriting.

h) Everyone was amazed by Gerards artwork.

i) Iains name was Scottish or Irish.

j) Where was Davids wallet?

10 marks

Where's my wallet?

Marks......... /10

Apostrophes

Challenge 3

 1 In this passage, the writer has got some apostrophes wrong or missed them out. Re-write the passage with the apostrophes used correctly.

> Jasons' new guitar was very expensive. It had been purchased by his wife Amanda, from a year's savings. The guitars special feature was that it was made from a very rare kind of wood. The woods' special qualities' included making it sound really loud and mellow. Jasons delight at seeing the guitar was great to see. His eyes' lit up as he could not believe that his wife had bought him such a fine thing. Amandas reaction was also one of joy as she liked to see Jason's smiling face. His playing on the guitar was fantastic – his fingers' sped up and down the frets' really quickly – Jasons playing improved greatly as a result of the fine guitar.

10 marks

Marks......... /10

Total marks .... /25　　　　How am I doing?

Silent Letters

G Grammar   P Punctuation   S Spelling

Challenge 1

1 Underline the silent letter in each of these words.

a) lamb

b) muscle

c) gnat

d) know

e) gnome

f) sign

g) rhyme

h) solemn

8 marks

Marks.......... /8

Challenge 2

1 In these sentences there is a word with a silent letter in it. Underline the word in each case.

a) Arms and legs are limbs.

b) The first scene in the play was the best.

c) Wednesday is the middle day of the week.

d) The cheetah is the fastest land animal in the world.

e) The girl had a knack for spotting the correct answer.

f) The teacher asked, has the cat got your tongue?

g) Do not kneel down in the mud.

h) Autumn is the wettest time.

i) Not everyone can afford a mortgage.

j) He must guess!

10 marks

Marks......... /10

Silent Letters

Challenge 3

S **1** In each of these sentences, the silent letter has been missed out of a word.

Write the missing letter in the space.

a) The bread crum___s were all over the floor.

b) The mountaineer clim___ed the peak.

c) S___issors are used to cut cloth and paper.

d) The hunters were thrown off the s___ent.

e) Another name for perfume is colo___ne.

f) The desi___n of the house was very clever.

g) Carol singers often ___nock in December.

h) In Scotland, a loc___ is a kind of lake.

i) Tom has a ___nack for maths.

j) My grandmother likes to ___nit sweaters.

k) The congregation sang a hym___ in church.

l) My colleag___e went to France to do some research.

m) Tom felt g___ilty because he hadn't done his homework.

n) The warrior carried a mighty s___ord.

o) A ___ren is a tiny bird.

15 marks

Marks......... /15

Total marks .... /33

How am I doing?

One-off and Irregular Spellings

G Grammar   P Punctuation   S Spelling

Challenge 1

1 Put a tick or a cross in the boxes to say whether the underlined word is spelled correctly in each of these sentences.

a) The man had severe <u>toothake</u>. ☐

b) The farmer owned hundreds of <u>acres</u> of land. ☐

c) They had to do it <u>agen</u> because they got it wrong first time. ☐

3 marks

2 Circle the word that is spelled correctly in these sentences.

a) His birthday is in **Febuary / February / Febury**.

b) We're going to **Eygpt / Egipt / Egypt**.

c) Nooria was a very **honest / onest / honist** girl.

3 marks

Marks.......... /6

Challenge 2

S **1** In these sentences, the underlined word has been spelled as it sounds, not as it should be spelled. Correct the spellings.

a) 'There is no correct <u>anser,</u>' said the teacher. _____

b) The runners did a <u>sirkit</u> of the track by running all the way round it. _____

c) The court case involved a famous <u>loyer.</u> _____

d) The day after Tuesday is <u>Wensday.</u> _____

e) '<u>Hoo</u> did that?' shouted the head teacher. _____

f) The children were too <u>yung</u> to go on the ride as it said 'Adults only'. _____

g) The ship sailed across the <u>oweshun</u> on its way to America. _____

h) The <u>erth</u> travels around the sun. _____

i) <u>Fizzical</u> activity is good for you. _____

j) The amazing jewel was a one-off – it was totally <u>yooneek.</u> _____

10 marks

Marks......... /10

One-off and Irregular Spellings

Challenge 3

1 A mnemonic is one way to remember tricky spellings.

> **Example** – a mnemonic for 'necessary' could be:
>
> <u>N</u>ever <u>E</u>at <u>C</u>risps <u>E</u>at <u>S</u>alad <u>S</u>andwiches <u>A</u>nd <u>R</u>emain <u>Y</u>oung

Make mnemonics for these one-off spellings.

Word	Mnemonic
a) Pharaoh	
b) Rhythm	
c) Vegetable	
d) Quote	
e) Depot	
f) Enough	
g) Straight	
h) Seize	
i) Thought	
j) Machine	

10 marks

Marks.........../10

Total marks ..../26

How am I doing?

Using a Thesaurus

Challenge 1

1 Circle the odd word out in each list.

a)   alien   foreigner   outlander   local

b)   thin   fat   slender   skinny

c)   big   massive   minuscule   massive

3 marks

Marks.......... /3

Challenge 2

1 Look at the words below. For each word, only one of the words in the list which follows it has a similar meaning. Underline the one which has the closest meaning.

a) delinquent – criminal / actor / policeman / sailor

b) delicacy – coarseness / roughness / fragility / strength

c) delightful – boring / horrible / enchanting / dry

d) delirious – crazed / shy / welcome / random

e) dejected – happy / ecstatic / sad / enthused

5 marks

2 Write down a synonym and an antonym for each of these words.

a) small   _____   _____

b) difficult   _____   _____

c) soak   _____   _____

6 marks

Marks.......... /11

Answers

Pages 4–5
Challenge 1
1 a) <u>use</u>less b) <u>slowly</u> c) <u>magic</u>ian

Challenge 2
1 a) hydrant
   b) eject
   c) dictated
   d) pedicure
   e) thermometer
   f) tripod
   g) predict
   h) reject
   i) thermostat
   j) hydrated

Challenge 3
1 a) Fear of spiders
   b) Able to read minds
   c) Someone's own signature
   d) Someone new to doing something
   e) Study of the earth

2 Many answers possible. Examples provided as a guide.
   a) Jane's arachnophobia meant that she could never dust the corners of the room.
   b) Sookie was telepathic and knew what everyone was thinking.
   c) The film star signed his autograph for a fan.
   d) The novice made many mistakes as he did not know what to do.
   e) Geography is my favourite subject at school.

Pages 6–7
Challenge 1
1 a) <u>inter</u>national b) <u>re</u>decorate
   c) <u>un</u>necessary d) <u>ir</u>regular e) <u>pre</u>view
   f) <u>dis</u>appear

Challenge 2
1 a) unbelievable
   b) unhealthy
   c) disagree
   d) dishonest
   e) misunderstand
   f) unfold
   g) disconnect
   h) untidy
   i) unpleasant

2 a) disagree
   b) disconnect
   c) dishonest
   d) unpleasant
   e) unfold
   f) untidy
   g) misunderstand
   h) unhealthy
   i) unbelievable

Challenge 3
1 a) redesigned
   b) international
   c) disentangled
   d) unveiled
   e) illiterate
   f) impolite
   g) inedible
   h) disproved
   i) dishonest
   j) misbehaving

Pages 8–9
Challenge 1
1 a) hesitant<u>ly</u>
   b) wish<u>ing</u>
   c) block<u>age</u>
   d) rea<u>der</u>
   e) excite<u>ment</u>
   f) close<u>ness</u>

Challenge 2
1 a) preventable
   b) blockage
   c) natural
   d) Italian
   e) molecular
   f) kingdom
   g) laughed
   h) hottest
   i) neighbourhood
   j) celebration

Challenge 3
1 a) government
   b) normally
   c) improvement
   d) readable
   e) spacious
   f) clueless
   g) motorised
   h) dangerous

2 b) regional
   d) wonderful
   f) magical
   c) customary
   e) basic
   g) foolish

Pages 10–11
Challenge 1
1 a) Paragraph b) Conclusion c) Introduction

Challenge 2
1 a) but
   b) and
   c) while
   d) After a while
   e) although
   f) but
   g) and
   h) So
   i) but
   j) Despite this

Challenge 3
1 Many answers possible. Examples provided as guidance of what is possible.
   Paragraph 1
   It banged! (Short sentence) The dark, gloomy and dull (3 adjectives) night was disrupted by a sudden firework explosion. What could it be? (Rhetorical question)
   Paragraph 2
   Despite the noise that had disturbed me, I was not put off in my exploration. (Complex sentence 1) I carried on, because I knew that the answer was out there somewhere. (Complex sentence 2) I was a bit scared, but I had to do this. (Opinion 1) I wasn't sure though – not totally sure (Opinion 2)
   Paragraph 3
   I carried on and walked around the corner, only to see what I had feared… (Ellipsis for a cliffhanger)

Pages 12–13

Challenge 1

1 a) amazing, armadillo, army

  b) bass, beautiful, boat

  c) card, cricket, crime

  d) track, tractor, tree

  e) laughing, lemon, limerick

Challenge 2

1 a) sleepwalk   e) having no colour

  b) stationary   f) new

  c) yes   g) two

  d) French (Cajun French)

Challenge 3

1 Bouquet; Clue; Debt; Egg; Igloo; Jewel; Kite; Mammoth; Night; Orange

Pages 14–15

Challenge 1

1 a) limerick   b) sonnet   c) poem

Challenge 2

1 a) Romance   d) Non-fiction

  b) Fantasy   e) Science fiction

  c) Autobiography

Challenge 3

1 Many answers possible. Examples provided as guidance only.

  a) The astronauts jumped into their rocket ship and set off through Galaxy X01 towards their base on the planet Zarg. Inside the ship, Captain Smith pressed the neo-transporter button and they beamed down to the surface.

  b) The wheels spun and rubber burnt as the two cars sped off across the industrial estate. Crime boss McMann was in the front, chased by Sergeant Wilkes of the crime squad. There was a sudden explosion as his car hit a barrel of oil outside a disused building.

  c) The owls hooted in the darkness and echoed across the graveyard. The wind blew and howled in harmony with the owls – and then something stirred….

Pages 16–17

Challenge 1

1 a) True   b) False   c) True

Challenge 2

1

Crime fiction	Policeman. Criminal. Element of mystery.
Cowboy stories	Horses. Wild West. Deserts. Ghost towns.
Comedy writing	Silliness. Exaggeration. Humour.
Fairy story	Handsome prince. Beautiful princess. Villain. Magic.
Autobiography	Real-life experiences. Personal thoughts and feelings. Often chronological.

Challenge 3

1 As the evening fell it began to get very cold, (Bad weather) and the growing twilight (Darkness) seemed to merge into one dark mistiness (Bad weather/darkness/power of nature) the gloom of the trees, oak, beech, and pine, though in the valleys which ran deep between the spurs of the hills, as we ascended through the Pass, the dark firs stood out here and there (Darkness/power of nature) against the background of late-lying snow (Bad weather/power of nature). Sometimes, as the road was cut through the pine woods that seemed in the darkness (Darkness) to be closing down upon us, great masses of greyness (Darkness), which here and there bestrewed the trees, produced a peculiarly weird and solemn effect, (Sense of mystery and fear/The supernatural/Power of nature) which carried on the thoughts and grim fancies engendered earlier in the evening, (Sense of mystery and fear) when the falling sunset threw into strange relief the ghost-like clouds (Bad weather/Sense of mystery and fear/The supernatural/Power of nature) which amongst the Carpathians seem to wind ceaselessly through the valleys (Power of nature). Sometimes the hills were so steep that, despite our driver's haste, the horses could only go slowly. I wished to get down and walk up them, as we do at home, but the driver would not hear of it. 'No, no', he said; 'you must not walk here; the dogs are too fierce'; (Sense of mystery and fear) and then he added, with what he evidently meant for grim pleasantry – for he looked round to catch the approving smile of the rest – 'and you may have enough of such matters before you go to sleep'. (Sense of mystery and fear) The only stop he would make was a moment's pause to light his lamps.

When it grew dark (Darkness) there seemed to be some excitement amongst the passengers, and they kept speaking to him, one after the other, as though urging him to further speed. He lashed the horses unmercifully with his long whip, and with wild cries of encouragement urged them on to further exertions. Then through the darkness (Darkness) I could see a sort of patch of grey light ahead of us, as though there were a cleft in the hills. (Sense of mystery and fear) The excitement of the passengers grew greater; the crazy coach rocked on its great leather springs, and swayed like a boat tossed on a stormy sea (Bad weather/Power of nature). I had to hold on.

Pages 18–19

Challenge 1

1 a) The word 'anxious' creates the feeling that the main character is uncertain about what he wants to do.

   b) The phrase 'Don't do it, Freddy!' creates the impression that the speaker is angry.

   c) By using the adjective 'clever' the writer makes the reader feel sympathy for the main character.

Challenge 2

1 a) … and <u>scorch</u> you with his fire.

   b) Naughty.

   c) Clamber.

   d) It suggests that their mother was right and they were wrong to under-estimate it by not listening.

Challenge 3

Different answers possible. Examples provided as guidance.

Point 1
The first way that the writer suggests that we should listen to the advice of others is seen when the mother speaks to the snowflakes strongly.

Quotation 1
'Now, listen', said their mother, 'don't you climb up any higher'.

Comment 1
The command 'Now, listen' is quite a strong and direct phrase, which implies that the advice that the mother is giving is important. It is followed by another imperative 'Don't…' which repeats the advice. Because of this, the advice must be important.

Point 2
The second way that the writer suggests that we should listen to the advice of others is seen when the writer describes their race to get to the sun.

Quotation 2
'They thought that they'd be back in time enough to go to bed.
But they found out that their mother wasn't quite the dunce they thought her'

Comment 2
The word 'thought' is a warning, because they didn't know what would happen – they just believed they would be OK. 'They found out' also sounds like a warning and it was too late – they were already melting in the sun by the time they discovered that their mother's advice was good.

Pages 20–21

Challenge 1

1 a) 5   b) 14   c) 2

Challenge 2

1

Acrostic	A poem where the first, last or other letters in a line spell out a word or phrase.
Epigram	A brief and memorable poem, designed to put over a key idea, often in a funny way.
Shape poem	Usually describes an object – and is shaped the same as the object that is being described.
Haiku	Originally a Japanese poem made of three lines and 17 syllables.
Ballad	A poem that tells a story.

Challenge 3

1 AABBA

2 Love

3 4

4 1st and 3rd and 2nd and 4th

5 It doesn't have any fixed pattern.

6 5

7 A sonnet.

8 The first, last or other letters in each line make a word.

9 ABBA

Pages 22–23

Challenge 1

1 a) True   b) True   c) False

Challenge 2

1 a) i) They are at a cinema.

      ii) They are talking about buying tickets and sweets/popcorn.

      iii) Yes

   a) i) At a doctor's or in a similar place where a medical examination happens.

      ii) Someone who has been playing sport and someone with medical knowledge.

      iii) They are talking about an injury, how it happened, how to check it – and what will happen because of it.

Challenge 3

1 a) ✓ b) ✗ c) ✓ d) ✓ e) ✗

Pages 24–25

Challenge 1

1 a) Fact   b) Opinion   c) Fact
   d) Fact   e) Opinion

Challenge 2

1. a) Fact
   b) Fact
   c) Opinion
   d) Opinion
   e) Opinion
   f) Opinion
   g) Opinion
   h) Fact
   i) Fact
   j) Fact
   k) Fact
   l) Opinion

Challenge 3

1. Many answers possible. Example provided as guidance of what might be possible.

I am 11 years old and I come from Basingstoke. I own a pair of red trainers. They are size 12. They cost £32.

Dark make-up suits my eyes. My favourite trainers are my red ones. My feet will grow. The trainers were quite expensive, because they're nicer than the blue ones.

Pages 26–27
Challenge 1

1. a) True   b) True   c) False

Challenge 2

1. a) Differences highlighted:
   Famous (female) country music singers were often well-known in the 1980s for wearing big wigs and cowboy boots; (.)(t)hey might have come from Nashville, Tennessee or Austin, Texas in the United States. Because of their (extreme) (unusual) appearance, they were seen as objects of fun outside (North) America, but in their own country they were seen as the height of (style) (fashion).
   b) Text 1 could be seen as more precisely written because it contains more detailed use of adjectives/it contains a stronger personal opinion.

Challenge 3

1. a) In both cases, some part of mankind had behaved badly.
   b) In text 1, it is the behaviour of one person that prompted revenge from a god, whereas in text 2, it is the behaviour of a group of people.
   c) They were both chosen to survive the flood. **OR** They were both seen as well-behaved.
   d) Deucalion uses a chest, Noah has an ark.

Page 28–29 – Progress Test 1

1.

Word		Prefix	Suffix	Root Word
a)	Unhappiness	un	ness	happy
b)	Forewarning	fore	ing	warn
c)	Rejigged	re	ed	jig

2. a) True   b) True   c) False

3. a) establishment
   b) decreased
   c) disappeared
   d) impossible
   e) extra-curricular
   f) destroyed
   g) tripod
   h) tabloid
   i) confusion

4. a) Formed in 1993/Formed in the North of England/Had many line-up changes.
   b) They are the premier European swamp'n'roll outfit.
   c) True
   d) It lists all the instruments that they can play, so this suggests they are versatile, because there are a lot of them.
   e) Both suggest that they are well-known because it mentions lots of places and countries where they have played.

5. a) A sonnet
   b) It has 14 lines (three quatrains and a rhyming couplet) and it has the theme of love.
   c) Dan
   d) Love
   e) For Dan knew he had more than gold. He had a love that would never grow old
   f) Three

6. running; snatched; dashed; looking; asked; replied; disappointed; realised; queried; purchased;

7. enraged; medical; packet; argued; contradicted

Pages 32–33
Challenge 1

1. a) **There** is the train!
   b) '**You're** not going out dressed like that!'
   c) **It's** impossible.
   d) The music is **too** loud!
   e) I don't **know** if Jay is coming with us.
   f) **They're** going home tomorrow.

Challenge 2

1. a) wring
   b) bald
   c) bazaar
   d) beach
   e) berry
   f) bread
   g) queue
   h) horde
   i) rite
   j) ark

Challenge 3

1.

Word	Correct? Yes or No	If incorrect, how should it be spelled?
by	No	buy
butt	No	but
course	Yes	
new	No	knew
practice	No	practise
pear	No	pair
rapped	No	wrapped
waste	No	waist
sea	No	see
whether	Yes	
seen	Yes	

Pages 34–35

Challenge 1 (Correct spelling provided.)

1. a) ✗ achieved
   b) ✗ aggressive
   c) ✓ appearance
   d) ✗ knowledge
   e) ✓ previous
   f) ✗ characters

Challenge 2

1. a) ✗ b) ✓ c) ✓ d) ✗ e) ✗
   f) ✓ g) ✗ h) ✓ i) ✓ j) ✗

2. assassination; believe; business; embarrassed; definitely

Challenge 3

The <u>politician</u> announced in his speech that there were going to be many changes. He <u>referred</u> to the mistakes made by the previous <u>government</u> and asked the audience to <u>remember</u> what a mess they had made of the country. He said that these new rules were <u>separate</u> from what the Prime Minister was going to announce later. He <u>hoped</u> that they would be <u>successful</u> in bringing back good times to the nation. The audience <u>were</u> surprised by his <u>bold</u> statements, but many decided to <u>wait</u> until they heard what the Prime Minister would say before making a judgement.

Pages 36–37

Challenge 1

1. a) One   b) More than one
   c) More than one   d) One
   e) More than one

Challenge 2

1. a) Brendan's taste in music was fantastic.
   b) Several people commented on how smart Declan's shirts were.
   c) Ken's video camera was the latest model.
   d) Willie's record shop was the friendliest in Ireland.
   e) Chris's (or Chris') post on the internet forum was liked by lots of people.
   f) Dunky's name was very strange, but it was a real name.
   g) No one understood Laura's handwriting.
   h) Everyone was amazed by Gerard's artwork.
   i) Iain's name was Scottish or Irish.
   j) Where was David's wallet?

Challenge 3

1. <u>Jason's</u> new guitar was very expensive. It had been purchased by his wife Amanda, from a year's savings. The <u>guitar's</u> special feature was that it was made from a very rare kind of wood. The <u>wood's</u> special <u>qualities</u> included making it sound really loud and mellow. <u>Jason's</u> delight at seeing the guitar was great to see. His <u>eyes</u> lit up as he could not believe that his wife had bought him such a fine thing. <u>Amanda's</u> reaction was also one of joy as she liked to see Jason's smiling face. His playing on the guitar was fantastic – his <u>fingers</u> sped up and down the <u>frets</u> really quickly – <u>Jason's</u> playing improved greatly as a result of the fine guitar.

Pages 38–39

Challenge 1

1. a) lam<u>b</u>
   b) mus<u>c</u>le
   c) <u>g</u>nat
   d) <u>k</u>now
   e) <u>g</u>nome
   f) si<u>g</u>n
   g) <u>rh</u>yme
   h) solem<u>n</u>

Challenge 2

1. a) <u>limb</u>s.
   b) <u>scene</u>.
   c) <u>Wednesday</u>.
   d) <u>cheetah</u>.
   e) <u>knack</u>.
   f) <u>tongue</u>.
   g) <u>kneel</u>.
   h) <u>Autumn</u>.
   i) <u>mortgage</u>.
   j) <u>guess</u>

Challenge 3

1. a) crumbs
   b) climbed
   c) Scissors
   d) scent
   e) cologne
   f) design
   g) knock
   h) loch
   i) knack
   j) knit
   k) hymn
   l) colleague
   m) guilty
   n) sword
   o) wren

Pages 40–41

Challenge 1

1. a) ✗ (toothache)   b) ✓   c) ✗ (again)

2. a) February   b) Egypt   c) honest

Challenge 2

1. a) answer
   b) circuit
   c) lawyer
   d) Wednesday
   e) Who
   f) young
   g) ocean
   h) Earth
   i) physical
   j) unique

Challenge 3

1. Many answers possible – examples given as suggestions only.
   a) Pharaoh – Poor Hydroplanes And Roads Always Operate Harshly
   b) Rhythm – Really Hard Yarns Test Hurt Mothers
   c) Vegetable – Victims Entice Glittery Engines Then Actresses Bash Large Engineers
   d) Quote – Quality Universities Obtain Tough Engineers
   e) Depot – Deaf Earworms Pursue Obsessive Teams
   f) Enough – Easy Natural Operators Understand Good Health
   g) Straight – Soldiers Test Recruits And Individuals Grow Huge Trees
   h) Seize – Slow Eyes Infect Zippy Ears
   i) Thought – Tricky Hollow Ones Understand Gorgeous Homemade Tractors
   j) Machine – Moving Amazing Chains Hides Individually New Eggs

Pages 42–43

Challenge 1

1   a)   local   b)   fat   c)   minuscule

Challenge 2

1   a)   delinquent – criminal
    b)   delicacy – fragility
    c)   delightful – enchanting
    d)   delirious – crazed
    e)   dejected – sad

2   Examples: a)   little; big   b)   hard; easy
                c)   drench; dry

Challenge 3

1   Many possible answers. Example given as guide to
    some possibilities.
    One <u>glorious</u> day, Robbie decided to go for a
    <u>lengthy</u> walk in the Scottish Highlands. Although
    the weather was <u>exceptional</u>, there was a <u>slight</u>
    chance of rain later in the day. The <u>enormous</u>
    mountains were on each side of him as he <u>paced</u>
    <u>frenetically</u> into the countryside. He could smell
    the <u>gorgeous</u> heather and enjoyed looking at
    the <u>spectacular</u> views in front of him. The sun
    shone <u>blazingly</u> above him and only a few <u>moody</u>
    clouds waited in the sky. That didn't last too long,
    however. A <u>fearful</u> wind started to grow and
    <u>intimidating</u> clouds built up. A few minutes later
    <u>sheets</u> of rain started to <u>plummet</u>.

Pages 44–47 – Progress Test 2

1   a)   True   b)   False   c)   True
2   a)   The criminal was <u>fined</u> a <u>week's</u> wages for
         breaking the law.
    b)   The <u>children's</u> day was spoiled because they
         got lost in the <u>maze</u>.
    c)   '<u>You</u> must be joking!' complained the
         <u>manager's</u> assistant.
    d)   The girls were <u>barred</u> from the shopping
         centre because of <u>Jemma's</u> behaviour.
    e)   <u>Robert's</u> car was regarded with jealousy by
         <u>some</u> people.
    f)   The <u>vampire's</u> fangs <u>seemed</u> to be sharp and
         pointy.g)   **Craig's stationary car was
         not going anywhere.**
    h)   All the supporters were <u>wailing</u> at the <u>referee's</u>
         decision.

3   a)   unhappy   b)   childish
    c)   unhelpful   d)   repeated
    e)   non-fiction   f)   comfortable
    g)   comical   h)   invisible
    i)   illogical   j)   showing
4   a)   viewed   b)   laziest
    c)   substandard   d)   rewrite
    e)   properly
5   a)   morning   b)   shake   c)   sighed

6   a)   singing   b)   hoping
    c)   performed   d)   walking
    e)   happened   f)   falling
    g)   disappeared   h)   worrying
    i)   cued   j)   started

7   Autobiography – A person's life story written by
    that person.
    Novel – A narrative that contains a fictional story.
    Biography – Someone's life story written by
    someone else.
    Letter – A piece of writing addressed to a particular
    person or people.

8   <u>There</u> was a <u>hole</u> in the <u>ceiling</u> where the <u>plumber</u>
    had put his foot through it. The rain started to
    <u>pour</u> <u>through</u> and the room got very wet indeed.
    Martyn and Emma <u>rang</u> the insurance company
    to try and solve the problem, but because it was
    <u>too</u> late at night, no one <u>answered</u>. To get rid of
    the smell of damp, Martyn sprayed <u>chlorine</u> on the
    floor, but it didn't really help.

Pages 48–49

Challenge 1

1   a)   True   b)   True   c)   False (it is
         theoretically possible, but so unlikely, that it
         should be seen as false!)

Challenge 2

1   a)   Darkness and storm / pitchy darkness /
         another darkened
    b)   Vivid flashes of lightning / dazzled my eyes /
         illuminating the lake / a vast sheet of fire / the
         preceding flash / enlightened / faint flashes
    c)   Faint flashes
    d)   The thunder burst with a terrific crash /
         dazzled my eyes / a vast sheet of fire/violent
         storm

Challenge 3

1   Many answers possible. Example given as a guide
    only as to how it might be done.
    The dark, gloomy sky hung above us. Lightning
    dazzled us with its momentary bursts and rays
    of light reflected off the menacing, threatening
    clouds. It was a smoky, scary scene which we
    couldn't escape.

Pages 50–51

Challenge 1

1   a)   True   c)   True   c)   False

Challenge 2

1   People who like cooking
2   People who like scary stories
3   Secondary schoolchildren
4   The shop manager
5   Someone who likes phones and cameras

Challenge 3

Many answers possible. Examples given as a guide only as to how they might be done.

1 a) Hi Dave – how's tricks? Doing anything Saturday? A true friend like you would come up town with me. If you don't, I'll tell your brother what you did with his sweets….

   b) Clare was thirteen, but that didn't mean that she didn't have a taste for exciting, dangerous and breath-stealing activities. She held tightly to the rope as she swung and wobbled in the wind, pressed to the side of the mountain. Rain lashed at her soaked clothes as she dared to look down…

Pages 52–53
Challenge 1

1 a) ✗ (not always, but often) b) ✓ c) ✓
2 and; but; because

Challenge 2

1

At first, I thought that I would never be able to get tickets for the concert because they were so expensive.
Fortunately, on the day that the tickets went on sale, I received a cheque through the post for over £200. I was delighted.
Having received this money, the next challenge was to make sure that I got online in time to get the best seats. So, at 9.15 sharp I logged on to the ticket sales website.
As I refreshed the web browser, the blood was rushing around my body – I'd never been so nervous – and then it happened. 'You have the VIP tickets in your basket. Please click on 'Next' to purchase them'.
As quickly as I could, I typed in my details and paid for them. When the screen came up which said I'd successfully purchased them, I ran around the room in delight!

Challenge 3

1 The first claims to have invented a mobile phone go back as far as 1908, but the people who were supposed to have invented it never actually produced one, as far as we are aware – they only made plans. // Later on in the century, hand-held radio transmitters and receivers were used in World War 2 and some phones made for using in cars were produced too, although they used up a great deal of power and were very expensive. // Further on, in the middle of the 20th century, engineers in Russia made a number of experimental mobile phones, some of which were supposed to be very small. These models were not very popular. // In addition, in America, some areas had their own networks, but again they were not very widely used as there weren't too many transmitters, making them only usable in a narrow area. // Before 1973, these types of mobile phones had to be used in vehicles – it was only in 1973 that the very first hand-held mobile phone was made, although it was enormous by today's standards. // Over the following years, the areas that could get reception were widened as big business found phones useful and put money into developing networks and improving the technology so that phones got smaller and smaller, resulting in the handsets that we have today.

Pages 54–55
Challenge 1

1 a) False   b) False   c) False

Challenge 2

1

Climax	This is the most exciting or suspense-filled part in the story
Exposition	This is the part at the start where the writer establishes the main character, settings and ideas
Falling Action	These are the events that happen before the resolution of the story
Resolution	This is the end of the story, where the outcome is revealed – it can be good, bad, both or neither!
Rising Action	This is the part where the initial events happen before the most exciting or significant parts of the writing. These parts contribute to suspense.

Challenge 3

Many alternatives possible. Examples given only as a guide to what might be possible.

1 The foreboding hills stretched out in front of the lonely figure. Above him gloomy clouds hung like vultures in the sky. From his back a piercing wind blew towards him like icy daggers. Underneath his feet, the hard ground lay, making it tiresome for him to continue his journey.

2 The rolling hills stretched out in front of the warm figure. Above him wispy clouds hung like candyfloss in the sky. From his back a soothing wind blew towards him like kisses. Underneath his feet, the soft ground lay, making it comfortable for him to continue his journey.

Pages 56–57

Challenge 1

1   a) ✓   b) ✗   c) ✓

Challenge 2

1

Number sections or paragraphs	Put things in the order in which you are going to write them.
Start at the end and work backwards	Know your ending and work backwards from there.
Write three paragraphs	Start, middle and end – and then build around that.
Mind maps	Visual mapping out of ideas, perhaps with colour-coding.
Character or topic arcs	Decide what is going to happen within each topic or to each character.
Jigsaw method	Write short parts of the whole text, then fit them together.

Challenge 3

Different answers possible. Examples given as a guide to what might be possible.

a) 1   Packing
    2   Going to the airport
    3   The flight
    4   Going through customs
    5   The hotel
    6   What we did

b)
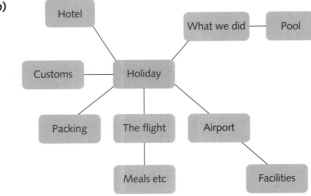

Pages 58–59

Challenge 1

1   a) False   b) True   c) True

Challenge 2

1   a)   It was his custom to go to the match.
    b)   They wanted to climb up to the summit. **Or –** They wanted to climb to the top of the hill.
    c)   The ruins of the abbey revealed interesting facts to the archaeologists.
    d)   Fred and Yasmin decided to return.
    e)   The darts player hit the target with precision.

f)   The donation to charity was not enough. **Or –** The donation to charity was not sufficient.

Challenge 3

1   Many different alternatives (73 words – a 5 mark example.)
Punk rock music started around the early 1970s, spreading around the world as a rebellion against mainstream rock. It was loud, fast and songs were short, not using many instruments. Many bands produced and sold their own songs. The word "punk" goes back in history but was re-used at this time. Several bands from the USA and UK were important. In 1977, the music became popular internationally and it created its own fashion. 60–75 words = 5 marks
76–85 words = 4 marks
86–95 words = 3 marks
96–105 words = 2 marks
106–110 words = 1 mark
111–121 words = 0 marks

Pages 60–61

Challenge 1

1   a)   They <u>are</u> the only ones who know what they're doing.
    b)   David <u>was</u> going to the match this afternoon.
    c)   Jane and Georgia <u>are</u> best friends.
    d)   Yusuf <u>ran</u> 6 miles last week.
    e)   The cats were <u>fighting</u> over a toy.

Challenge 2

1   a)   finished.
    b)   mistake.
    c)   Double-check.
    d)   hard.
    e)   loud.
    f)   spell-checker.
    g)   dictionary.
    h)   backwards.
    i)   checklist.
    j)   someone.

Challenge 3

When I came <u>to</u> again, I <u>was</u> sitting under an <u>oa</u>k tree, on the grass, with a whole beautiful and broad country landscape all to myself—nearly. Not entirely; for there was a fellow on <u>a</u> horse, looking down at me—a fellow fresh out <u>of</u> a picture-book. He was in old-time iron armour from head to <u>heel</u>, with a helmet on his head the shape of a nail-keg with slits in <u>it and</u> he had a shield, and a sword, and a prodigious <u>spear and</u> his horse <u>had</u> armour on too, and a steel horn projecting from his forehead, and gorgeous <u>red</u> and green silk trappings that hung down all around him like a bed quilt, nearly to the ground.

1 **a)** False   **b)** True   **c)** True
2 **a)**   **i)** A limerick
     ii) Two from: It has five lines and is AABBA./
     It is humorous./Its last line is a punchline.
   b) She is messy./She is untidy./She cannot face
     up to cleaning.
   c) She is a young lady./She lives in a house. She
     picked up a duster./She put down a duster.
3 **a)** It is a long-distance walking path./It runs from
     Milngavie to Fort William./It is approximately
     96 miles long./It is in Scotland.
   b) It is the hardest long-distance path to walk in
     the UK.
   c)   **i)** True
     ii) It mentions 'beautiful countryside', but
     talks about an 'urban area' (implying it
     isn't pretty) and it talks of and describes a
     'difficult stretch'.
   d) It is difficult because – it goes through wild
     and remote land – it covers a very bleak area
     which might be dangerous in poor weather –
     there is a 'big climb'.
4 **a)** They are <u>our</u> seats.
   b) <u>We're</u> going to Florida for our holidays.
   c) There was a <u>sale</u> on at the clothing shop.
5 **a)** numb   **b)** obscene
   c) handkerchief   **d)** gnome
   e) echo   **f)** knapsack
   g) condemn   **h)** listening
6 **a)** Fact   **b)** Opinion
   c) Opinion   **d)** Fact
   e) Opinion

7 Many different alternatives possible. One example
given as a guide to what might be done.

Jagram walked <u>speedily</u> towards the <u>enormous</u>
door, because he knew that the teacher was
waiting inside. He <u>tip-toed</u> into the classroom
and sat down <u>nervously</u> at his desk. It was his
least favourite lesson, so he had brought some
<u>delicious</u> sweets to pass the time. <u>Sneakily</u>, he
took one out of his pocket and <u>inched</u> it towards
his mouth, hoping that the teacher would not
see him. Unluckily for Jagram the teacher <u>noticed</u>
him and told him to hand over the sweets. He
took them off him <u>immediately</u>. <u>Subsequently</u>, the
teacher handed them out to everyone else in the
class….

Challenge 1
1 **a)** ✓   **b)** ✓   **f)** ✓

Challenge 2

1

2nd person singular	You are playing	You were playing
3rd person singular	He/she/it is playing	He/she/it was playing
1st person plural	We are playing	We were playing
2nd person plural	You are playing	You were playing
3rd person plural	They are playing	They were playing

2

Present Simple	I play
Present Continuous	I am playing
Present Perfect	I have played
Past Continuous	I was playing
Past Perfect	I had played
Past Perfect Continuous	I had been playing
Future	I will play
Future Continuous	I will be playing
Future Perfect Continuous	I will have been playing

Challenge 3
1 Different versions of the past tense are indicated.
Either form is acceptable, but should be used
appropriately throughout.

I <u>was buying/bought</u> some new shoes. I <u>was paying/
paid</u> for them with my pocket money. I <u>was taking/
took</u> them to show my friends. My friends <u>were
looking/looked</u> at the shoes while we <u>were drinking/
drank</u> coffee in the coffee shop. We <u>were walking/
walked</u> to the bus station.

2 **a)** Chloe
   b) Active
   c) The wall was painted (by Chloe).

Challenge 1
1 **a)** will
   b) will
   c) shall
2 **a)** far   **b)** confidently   **c)** quickly

Challenge 2
1 **a)** She played happily.
   b) She sang beautifully.
   c) He spoke to her honestly.
   d) It was shining strongly.
   e) We looked at each other sadly.

2 a) <u>As soon as</u> it arrived, we ate the food.

b) James got up early <u>yesterday morning</u>.

Challenge 3

1 Many different answers possible. Example given as a guide only.

Mary walked <u>purposefully</u> towards the shop. <u>Unfortunately</u> it was shut, but that didn't stop Mary. She knocked <u>loudly</u> on the door and shouted <u>urgently</u> at the upstairs window. A window <u>slowly</u> opened and a head <u>lazily</u> peered out.

'Who's that?' said a voice, <u>drowsily</u>.

'It's one of your customers!' replied Mary <u>impatiently</u>. 'It's past your opening time. Why aren't you open?'

There was no reply, but the window was <u>quickly</u> closed and there were sounds of movement going on, before a figure appeared at the shop door. There was the sound of shuffling keys and the lock <u>creakily</u> turned and the door opened.

'I'm sorry – my alarm didn't go off. Please come in'. Mary shrugged her shoulders <u>sharply</u> and strode <u>confidently</u> into the shop.

'What would you like?' asked the shop assistant <u>politely</u>.

'Have you got any chocolate biscuits?' said Mary, while fiddling <u>clumsily</u> in her bag for her purse.

'I'm sorry', replied the assistant <u>hesitantly</u> – 'We're a chemists…'.

Pages 70–71
Challenge 1
1 a) ✓   b) ✗   c) ✓

Challenge 2
1 a) ✗ b) ✓ c) ✓ d) ✗ e) ✓ f) ✗
g) ✓ h) ✓ i) ✗

Challenge 3
1 a) Jessica, an excellent student, is also a trainee nurse.

b) Volker watched a film, *Grease*, last week.

c) John was shocked when he saw his former boss, Eric, in the shop.

d) When I saw Mr Tingle, my old Chemistry teacher, I immediately thought about my time at school.

e) This idea, how to use commas, can be a tricky concept in English.

f) There goes Scott, a great footballer, who also serves on the school council.

g) Tiny, my oldest pet, is a Yorkshire Terrier with brown and black fur.

h) Amy, the girl with her hair in a bun, is in my maths class.

i) This dress, made of silk and cotton, was given to me by my best friend.

j) My goldfish, Winona, has been acting strangely for a while.

2 a) The village was very quiet, <u>which suited him fine</u>.

b) She put on her hat, <u>which was blue</u>.

Pages 72–73
Challenge 1
1 ✓ Hyphen **2** ✓ Dashes **3** ✓ Hyphen

Challenge 2
1 a) James Smith – our clever student – is standing for the Youth Parliament again.

b) Will he – can he – win the election?

c) James Smith – footballer, head boy and general brainbox – is standing for the school council too.

d) Posters, marker pens, drawing pins – everything is ready.

e) There was only one thing left to do – build a treehouse!

2 a) We were stuck in the hold-up on the M25.

b) I like self-assembly tables.

c) I also like off-the-peg suits.

d) He acted in self-defence.

e) I like seventeenth-century houses.

Challenge 3
1 a) ✓ b) ✓ c) ✗ d) ✗ e) ✓

2 a) My mother-in-law is coming for dinner tomorrow.

b) The children – those who are taking part in the walk – will raise a lot of money for charity.

c) It's all over now – just wait and see!

d) My sister is twenty-three years old.

e) My friends (Helen and Jo) are coming on holiday with me.

Pages 74–75
Challenge 1
1 a) ✓   b) ✗   c) ✓

Challenge 2
1 a) ✗ b) ✓ c) ✓ d) ✗ e) ✓ f) ✓
g) ✗ h) ✗ i) ✓

Challenge 3
1 a) My guitar playing is excellent; I will join a group.

b) My camera is broken; I have another one.

c) The market is shut; I have no food.

d) The weather is cold; it is snowing.

e) The fire is on; it is not very warm.

Answers 2. a) and b) have many alternatives. These are intended as a guide only.

2 a) The rain is pouring; I am going to get wet.

b) The television has broken; I cannot watch the football.

3 a) There are two choices at this moment in time: run away or give up.

b) This house has everything I need: three bedrooms, a fitted kitchen and a loft studio.

c) Paul wanted to know why I didn't answer his

text: I hadn't received it.

   d) These are my favourite foods: chips, chips, chips and chips!

   e) I bought a lot of meat at the supermarket: beef, turkey, chicken and lamb.

Answers 4. a) and b) have many alternatives. These are intended as a guide only.

4 **a)** I have many hobbies: playing music, taking photographs and sleeping!

   b) He has been to many countries: Australia, Thailand, France, Spain and Canada.

Pages 76–77
Challenge 1
1 At weekends people enjoy – going shopping
He is from – the older part of town
I adopted – a timid black and white kitten

2 **a)** They have bought <u>a lovely new cottage</u>.
   b) <u>My six children</u> go to school here.
   c) <u>Those two guitars</u> are mine.

Challenge 2
2 **a)** Yes **b)** No **c)** Yes **d)** No **e)** No
   f) No **g)** No **h)** No **i)** No **j)** Yes

Challenge 3
Many answers possible. These are intended only as a guide.
1 **a)** <u>Our cat</u> is happy.
   b) <u>Their cat</u> is sad.
   c) <u>Our big dog</u> is angry.
   d) <u>The slobbering cat</u> needs a vet.
   e) <u>The strange goldfish</u> swam around.
   f) <u>The cat on the mat</u> purred.
   g) <u>The dog on the roof</u> barked.
   h) <u>The dog to love</u>, belongs to us.
   i) <u>The cat that chases dogs</u> is theirs.
   j) <u>The cat purring for catnip</u> is healthy.

Pages 78–81 – Progress Test 4
1 **a)** I ate food.   **b)** I ran quickly
   c) I played happily.
2 **a)** Luckily
   b) quickly
   c) greedily
   d) fitfully
   e) slowly

3 **a)** will/shall
   b) can
   c) shall/will
4 **a)** The boy and his sister
   b) Sophie
   c) liked
   d) Active voice
   e) Relative pronoun

5 Many answers possible. An example is given as guide only.

I got up wearily and stumbled to the bathroom. I could have gone back to bed – or I could have got dressed – but I jumped in the bath instead. Unfortunately, (How silly am I?) there was no water in it at the time, so I had to wait for it to fill up. I waited; the water filled the bath. It was cold, so I turned the cold tap off and turned the hot tap up. There was no change: disaster! I could have cried, but I didn't bother. I got out and went lazily downstairs to make a drink instead.

6 **a)** William Wordsworth
   b) William Shakespeare
   c) John Keats
7 **a)** It is ~~absolutely~~ essential that you bring your umbrella.
   b) The ~~actual~~ facts speak for themselves.
   c) Make sure you do some ~~advance~~ planning.
   d) A ~~anonymous~~ stranger just spoke to me in the street.
   e) We should collaborate ~~together~~ on this.
   f) We could also co-operate ~~together~~.
   g) I hope to ~~entirely~~ eliminate the ants in the cellar.
   h) I hope I don't get ~~harmful~~ injuries from taking part.
   i) That is a good ~~illustrated~~ drawing.
   j) We should postpone this ~~until later~~.

8 **a)** AABB
   b) The poem says that the grasshopper hurt the elephant by stepping on his toe, but it's obvious that an elephant wouldn't feel a grasshopper standing on its toe.

9 <u>Many pieces</u> of pottery were made in North <u>Staffordshire</u>, because this was the home of the pottery industry. <u>It</u> was started here by Josiah Wedgwood and others several centuries ago. Small villages <u>became</u> towns, for example Burslem and <u>Hanley</u>. Industrial processes <u>were</u> used to speed up the <u>process</u> of making pottery. The local area was well-connected to the rest of the country via the growing canal <u>network</u>. As a result of this, goods <u>could</u> be shipped far and wide without breaking.

Progress Test Charts

Progress Test 1

Q	Topic	✓ or ✗	See page
1	Prefixes Suffixes Root words		6 8 4
2	Structure and Organisation		10
3	Prefixes Suffixes		6 8
4	Picking Out and Commenting on Details Retrieving Information		18 22
5	Types of Poetry		20
6	Suffixes		8
7	Prefixes Suffixes Root words		6 8 4

Progress Test 2

Q	Topic	✓ or ✗	See page
1	Prefixes		6
2	Homophones Apostrophes		32 36
3	Prefixes Suffixes		6 8
4	Prefixes Suffixes Root words		6 8 4
5	Homophones		32
6	Suffixes Root words		8 4
7	Prose Genres		14
8	Silent Letters Homophones One-off and Irregular Spellings		38 32 40

Progress Test 3

Q	Topic	✓ or ✗	See page
1	Paragraphs Using Dictionaries Types of Poetry		52 12 20
2	Types of Poetry		20
3	Picking Out and Commenting on Details Retrieving Information Fact and Opinion		18 22 24
4	Homophones		32
5	Silent Letters		38
6	Fact and Opinion		24
7	Using a Thesaurus		42

Progress Test 4

Q	Topic	✓ or ✗	See page
1	Verbs		66
2	Adverbs and Modal Verbs		68
3	Adverbs and Modal Verbs		68
4	Verbs Commas		66 70
5	Paragraphs Verbs Adverbs and Modal Verbs Commas Hyphens, Dashes and Brackets Semi-colons and Colons		52 66 68 70 72 74
6	Themes and conventions		16
7	Précis		58
8	Types of Poetry		20
9	Proof-reading		60

What am I doing well in? _____

_____

What do I need to improve? _____

_____

Using a Thesaurus

Challenge 3

1   Use a thesaurus to improve the vocabulary in the
    passage, by replacing all the underlined words.
    (The meanings do not have to be exact, if you
    want to change the tone of the piece.)

One <u>fine</u> day, Robbie decided to go for a
<u>long</u> walk in the Scottish Highlands.
Although the weather was <u>good</u>, there was
a <u>small</u> chance of rain later in the day. The <u>big</u> mountains were
on each side of him as he <u>walked</u> <u>quickly</u> into the countryside.
He could smell the <u>pretty</u> heather and enjoyed looking at the
<u>good</u> views in front of him. The sun shone <u>brightly</u> above him
and only a few <u>dark</u> clouds waited in the sky. That didn't last too
long, however. A <u>strong</u> wind started to grow and <u>big</u> clouds built
up. A few minutes later <u>a lot</u> of rain started to <u>fall down</u>.

15 marks

Marks......... /15

Total marks .... /29   How am I doing?

43

1 State whether each of these sentences is **true** or **false**.

a) The prefix 'inter' means 'between'. _____

b) The prefix 're' means 'before'. _____

c) The prefix 'pre' means 'before'. _____

3 marks

GPS **2** In each of these sentences there is a homophone spelling mistake and a missing apostrophe. Correct the spelling and the apostrophe.

a) The criminal was find a weeks wages for breaking the law.

_____

b) The childrens day was spoiled because they got lost in the man-made fun maize.

_____

c) 'Ewe must be joking!' complained the managers assistant.

_____

d) The girls were bard from the shopping centre because of Jemmas behaviour.

_____

e) Roberts car was regarded with jealousy by sum people.

_____

f) The vampires fangs seamed to be sharp and pointy.

_____

g) Craigs stationery car was not going anywhere.

_____

h) All the supporters were whaling at the referees decision.

_____

16 marks

3 The underlined words in these sentences have something wrong with their prefix or suffix. Change the underlined words so that the sentences make sense.

a) The man was <u>dishappy</u> because he had lost his wallet.

_____

b) The boy's behaviour was very immature and <u>childness</u>.

_____

c) The directions must have been very <u>mishelpful</u>, because they got lost. _____

d) They <u>depeated</u> their homework because they had done it wrong. _____

e) There were lots of <u>unfiction</u> texts in the library.

_____

f) The seats were <u>comfortness</u> on the train.

_____

g) The warm-up act at the show was very <u>comicable</u>.

_____

h) Wearing camouflage made the soldiers almost <u>unvisible</u>.

_____

i) The answer seemed completely <u>unlogical</u>.

_____

j) The cinema was <u>showed</u> the blockbuster film.

_____

10 marks

4 In this passage, there are a number of root words underlined, but they are missing their prefix or suffix, for the sentence to make sense. Add an appropriate prefix or suffix to make the passage make sense. Change the spelling of the root word if necessary.

Ed was <u>view</u> _____ by many of his classmates as the <u>lazy</u>_____ boy in the school, because he rarely did his homework – and when he did, it was of a _____ <u>standard</u> quality. The teacher made him _____ <u>write</u> several pieces of work, because they hadn't been done <u>proper</u> _____ first time.

5 marks

G **5** Underline the correct homophone in each example.

   a) The game will take place in the **mourning/morning**.

   b) '**Sheikh/Shake** it off!' was the advice given.

   c) 'I can't,' she **side/sighed**.

3 marks

6 Complete the passage by adding the missing suffixes. Change the spelling of the end of the root word where needed.

Emily was sing_____ in a competition and was hope _____ to win. She perform_____ her warm-up exercises and was walk_____ onto the stage, when a strange thing happen_____. The curtain began fall_____ in front of her and the audience disappear_____! Without worry_____ she cue_____ the band and they start_____ playing anyway.

10 marks

7 Draw lines to match each prose genre to its description.

Genre

Autobiography

Novel

Biography

Letter

Description

A piece of writing addressed to a particular person or people.

A person's life story written by that person.

A narrative that contains a fictional story.

Someone's life story written by someone else.

4 marks

GPS 8 In this passage, the following things need to be corrected:

- missing silent letters
- homophone/spelling mistakes

Find the mistakes and re-write the corrected version of the passage in the space below.

Their was a whole in the sealing where the plumer had put his foot through it. The rain started to pore threw and the room got very wet indeed. Martyn and Emma wrang the insurance company to try and solve the problem, but because it was to late at night, no one ansered. To get rid of the smell of damp, Martyn sprayed clorine on the floor, but it didn't really help.

_____

_____

_____

_____

_____

_____

_____

_____

_____

_____

10 marks

Marks.........../61

Learning from Other Writers

G Grammar   P Punctuation   S Spelling

Challenge 1

1 State whether each of these sentences is **true** or **false**.

a) You can use other writers as style models. _____

b) Some writers like to use the style of other writers to improve their own writing. _____

c) Some writers like to copy other writers because they want to be friends with them. _____

3 marks

Marks.......... /3

Challenge 2

1 Read the passage below and answer the questions that follow.

From 'Frankenstein' by Mary Shelley

I quitted my seat, and walked on, although the darkness and storm increased every minute, and the thunder burst with a terrific crash over my head. It was echoed from Saleve, the Juras, and the Alps of Savoy; vivid flashes of lightning dazzled my eyes, illuminating the lake, making it appear like a vast sheet of fire; then for an instant everything seemed of a pitchy darkness, until the eye recovered itself from the preceding flash. The storm, as is often the case in Switzerland, appeared at once in various parts of the heavens. The most violent storm hung exactly north of the town, over the part of the lake which lies between the promontory of Belrive and the village of Copet. Another storm enlightened Jura with faint flashes; and another darkened and sometimes disclosed the Mole, a peaked mountain to the east of the lake.

a) Find two examples of phrases to do with dark.

_____

2 marks

b) Find two examples of phrases to do with light.

_____

2 marks

c) Find an example of alliteration. _____

1 mark

d) Find two examples of phrases to do with violence.

_____

2 marks

Marks.......... /7

Learning from Other Writers

Challenge 3

GPS 1 Now write your own description of a storm, in the style of Mary Shelley. Include the following features:

- Two words to do with dark
- Two words to do with light
- Alliteration
- Two words to do with violence

2 marks

2 marks

1 mark

2 marks

_____

_____

_____

_____

_____

_____

_____

_____

_____

_____

_____

_____

_____

_____

_____

_____

_____

_____

Marks.........../7

Total marks .... /17   How am I doing?

Audience and Purpose

Challenge 1

1 State whether each of these sentences is **true** or **false**.

a) All texts are written for some sort of audience. _____

b) There can be more than one purpose for a text. _____

c) Texts always have a single audience. _____

3 marks

Marks.......... /3

Challenge 2

1 Who might be the main audience for these texts? Tick the most likely answer in each case.

a) A recipe book

Railway enthusiasts ☐   People who like cooking ☐

Teachers ☐   Children ☐

b) A gothic novel

People who like romance ☐   People who like facts ☐

People who like scary stories ☐   People who like Information ☐

c) A GCSE biology text book

Secondary schoolchildren ☐   English teachers ☐

Primary schoolchildren ☐   Professors of biology ☐

d) A letter of complaint about faulty goods from a shop

The government ☐   The police ☐

The shop manager ☐   The advertisers ☐

e) A gadget magazine

Someone who likes trains ☐   Someone who likes food ☐

Someone who likes phones and cameras ☐   Someone who likes astronomy ☐

5 marks

Marks.......... /5

Audience and Purpose

Challenge 3

GPS **1** Write a paragraph for each of the following types of audiences and purposes. Make sure you include the features listed.

a)

Audience and task	Purpose	Features to include
An email to a friend	To persuade them to go shopping with you	• Informal language • Two different persuasive techniques

_____

_____

_____

_____

_____

_____

_____

3 marks

b)

Audience and task	Purpose	Features to include
An opening paragraph from an adventure story for a teenage audience	To entertain	• Three exciting verbs • Two exaggerated adjectives

_____

_____

_____

_____

_____

_____

_____

5 marks

Marks............/8

Total marks .... /16   How am I doing?

Paragraphs

Challenge 1

1 Put a tick or cross in the boxes to say whether each sentence is correct.

   a) A topic sentence is always the first sentence in a paragraph. ☐

   b) Conjunctions can link ideas in one sentence with ideas in another. ☐

   c) Conjunctions can join two ideas in one sentence. ☐

         3 marks

2 Circle the conjunctions.

| and | under | but | because | down | new |

3 marks

Marks.......... /6

Challenge 2

1 Number these short paragraphs 1–5 to put them in the correct order.

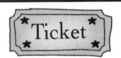
Ticket

Paragraphs	Order
Having received this money, the next challenge was to make sure that I got online in time to get the best seats. So, at 9.15 sharp I logged on to the ticket sales website.	
At first, I thought that I would never be able to get tickets for the concert because they were so expensive.	
As I refreshed the web browser, the blood was rushing around my body – I'd never been so nervous – and then it happened. 'You have the VIP tickets in your basket. Please click on "Next" to purchase them.'	
As quickly as I could, I typed in my details and paid for them. When the screen came up which said I'd successfully purchased them, I ran around the room in delight!	
Fortunately, on the day that the tickets went on sale, I received a cheque through the post for over £200. I was delighted.	

5 marks

Marks.......... /5

Paragraphs

Challenge 3

1 Read this passage and mark using the marker **'//'** where each paragraph starts.

The first claims to have invented a mobile phone go back as far as 1908, but the people who were supposed to have invented it never actually produced one, as far as we are aware – they only made plans. Later on in the century, hand-held radio transmitters and receivers were used in World War 2 and some phones made for using in cars were produced too, although they used up a great deal of power and were very expensive. Further on, in the middle of the 20th century, engineers in Russia made a number of experimental mobile phones, some of which were supposed to be very small. These models were not very popular. In addition, in America, some areas had their own networks, but again they were not very widely used as there weren't too many transmitters, making them only usable in a narrow area. Before 1973, these types of mobile phones had to be used in vehicles – it was only in 1973 that the very first hand-held mobile phone was made, although it was enormous by today's standards. Over the following years, the areas that could get reception were widened as big business found phones useful and put money into developing networks and improving the technology so that phones got smaller and smaller, resulting in the handsets that we have today.

5 marks

Marks.......... /5

Total marks .... /16

How am I doing?

Settings, Character and Plot

Challenge 1

1 State whether each of these sentences is **true** or **false**.

a) A setting has to be a real place.

_____

b) Characters are always based on real people. _____

c) Stories must always be written in the past tense. _____

3 marks

Marks........../3

Challenge 2

1 Draw lines to match the parts of a story with their descriptions.

Part of story	Description
Climax	These are the events that happen before the resolution of the story.
Exposition	This is the end of the story, where the outcome is revealed – it can be good, bad, both or neither!
Falling Action	This is the part at the start where the writer establishes the main character, settings and ideas.
Resolution	This is the part where the initial events happen before the most exciting or significant parts of the writing. These parts contribute to suspense.
Rising Action	This is the most exciting or suspense-filled part in the story.

5 marks

Marks........../5

Settings, Character and Plot

Challenge 3

1   Fill in the gaps to create a mysterious, scary setting.

> The _____ hills stretched out in front of the _____ figure. Above him _____ clouds hung like _____ in the sky. From his back a _____ wind blew towards him like _____. Underneath his feet, the _____ ground lay, making it _____ for him to continue his journey.

8 marks

2   Now fill in the gaps again, but this time, choose words that create a happy, more cheerful setting.

> The _____ hills stretched out in front of the _____ figure. Above him _____ clouds hung like _____ in the sky. From his back a _____ wind blew towards him like _____. Underneath his feet, the _____ ground lay, making it _____ for him to continue his journey.

8 marks

Marks......... /16

Organising and Planning Your Writing

Challenge 1

1 Put a tick or cross in the boxes to show whether these statements are correct.

a) A style model can be another piece of writing that you use to base your ideas on. ☐

b) A mind map is not an appropriate plan. ☐

c) Making a list of ideas is an appropriate way of planning in some circumstances. ☐

3 marks

Marks.........../3

Challenge 2

1 Match up the names of the planning methods with their descriptions.

Planning method	Description
Number sections or paragraphs	Visual mapping out of ideas, perhaps with colour-coding.
Start at the end and work backwards	Decide what is going to happen within each topic or to each character.
Write three paragraphs	Know your ending and work backwards from there.
Mind maps	Write short parts of the whole text, then fit them together.
Character or topic arcs	Put things in the order in which you are going to write them.
Jigsaw method	Start, middle and end – and then build around that.

6 marks

Marks.........../6

Organising and Planning Your Writing

Challenge 3

1 Make two different plans for the following task:

> Write an account of a holiday that you have been on and enjoyed, to be published in a travel magazine. It needs to be six paragraphs long.

a) **Planning Method 1**

Make a plan for this task, by making a numbered list of what goes in each paragraph.

1. _____   4. _____

2. _____   5. _____

3. _____   6. _____

6 marks

b) **Planning Method 2**

Make a plan for this task by drawing a mind-map in the box below.

6 marks

Marks.........../12

Total marks .... /21   How am I doing?

Précis

Challenge 1

1 State whether these sentences are **true** or **false**.

a) Précis means to make a piece of writing longer and more detailed. _____

b) Précis means to do a shortened version of a longer piece of writing. _____

c) Précis skills are useful when making notes. _____

3 marks

Marks.......... /3

Challenge 2

GPS **1** The following sentences have words that could be removed to make the sentence shorter. Write a shortened version of each sentence.

a) It was usually his custom to go to the match.

_____

_____

b) They wanted to climb up to the summit at the very top of the hill.

_____

_____

c) The destroyed ruins of the abbey revealed many interesting facts to the archaeologists.

_____

_____

d) Fred and Yasmin decided to return again for a second time.

_____

_____

e) The darts player hit the target with precise precision.

_____

_____

Précis

f) The donation to charity was not sufficient enough.

_____

_____

6 marks

Marks.......... /6

Challenge 3

GPS 1 Read the passage below and write a shorter version on a separate piece of paper.

> Punk rock is a style of rock music that developed between 1969 and 1976 in the United States, United Kingdom, and other parts of the world. Punk rock bands rebelled against mainstream 1970s rock. Punk bands created fast, loud music, typically with short songs, not many instruments, and often controversial lyrics. Many bands produced recordings themselves and distributed them themselves.
>
> The term 'punk' was first used in relation to rock music by some American writers in the early 1970s but the word itself actually goes back to Elizabethan England to describe someone of a poor reputation. By 1976, bands such as The Clash and The Damned in London, and Television, Patti Smith, and the Ramones in New York City were recognized as the most important bands in a new movement. The following year saw punk rock spread around the world, and it had a major impact in the United Kingdom. Punk style developed, expressing youthful rebellion and shown by distinctive styles of clothing and decoration (ranging from rude and offensive T-shirts, leather jackets, Mohican haircuts, to safety pins and tartan trousers).

5 marks

Marks.......... /5

Total marks .... /14   How am I doing?

Proof-reading

Challenge 1

GS) **1** Circle the mistakes in these sentences and correct them.

a) They is the only ones who know what they're doing. _____

b) David were going to the match this afternoon. _____

c) Jane and Georgia is best friends. _____

d) Yusuf runs six miles last week. _____

e) The cats were fight over a toy. _____

5 marks

Marks.......... /5

Challenge 2

1 Here are some pieces of advice on proof-reading.
Fill in the gaps with the words from the list below.

| dictionary | mistake | spell-checker | Double-check | backwards |

| hard | checklist | finished | someone | loud |

a) Don't check straight after you've _____.

b) Look for one type of error or _____ at a time.

c) _____ facts, figures, and proper names.

d) Check a _____ copy.

e) Read your text out _____.

f) Use a _____ if working on a computer.

g) Use a _____.

h) Read your text _____.

i) Create your own proof-reading

_____.

j) Ask _____ else to proof-read
your text after you have checked it.

10 marks

Marks........ /10

Proof-reading

Challenge 3

GPS **1** Read this passage and correct the mistakes in it. Re-write the passage underneath.

> Adapted from 'A Yankee in King Arthur's Court' by Mark Twain
>
> When I came too again, I were sitting under an oke tree, on the grass, with a whole beautiful and broad country landscape all to myself—nearly. Not entirely; for there was a fellow on an horse, looking down at me—a fellow fresh out off a picture-book. He was in old-time iron armour from head to heal, with a helmet on his head the shape of a nail-keg with slits in it. and he had a shield, and a sword, and a prodigious spear? and his horse has armour on too, and a steel horn projecting from his forehead, and gorgeous redd and green silk trappings that hung down all around him like a bed quilt, nearly to the ground.

10 marks

Marks........ /10

Total marks .... /25

How am I doing?

Progress Test 3

1   Say whether each of these statements is **true** or **false**.

   a)   A paragraph needs to be five sentences long. _____

   b)   'Radio' comes before 'Random' in the dictionary. _____

   c)   A limerick is a type of poem. _____

3 marks

2   Read the poem and answer the questions that follow.

> There was a young lady called Jess
> Whose house was seen as a mess –
> She picked up a duster
> With all the strength she could muster
> But put it down in fear and distress!

   a) i)   What kind of poem is this? _____

1 mark

      ii)   Give two reasons why you know it is this type of poem.

      _____

      _____

2 marks

   b)   What does this poem suggest about the character of Jess?

   _____

1 mark

   c)   Give one fact about Jess.

   _____

1 mark

3   Read this passage and answer the questions that follow.

> The West Highland Way is a long-distance walking path which runs from Milngavie, just outside Glasgow, to Fort William approximately 96 miles further north in Scotland. It is the hardest long-distance path to walk in the UK.
>
> The walk begins in an urban area but quickly turns into beautiful countryside near the shores of Loch Lomond. There is a somewhat difficult stretch along the eastern side of Loch Lomond, where the walker needs to avoid lots of tree roots and slippery rocks.

North of Loch Lomond, the walk starts to venture into the wild and remote Highlands. One part of the walk, which is not advisable in poor weather, is the walk over Rannoch Moor, one of the bleakest and most remote parts of Scotland.

After that, there is a big climb up the Devil's Staircase path on the way to Glencoe and then the route takes the walker onwards to Fort William. The end of the path is marked by a statue and a street display in Fort William, where photographs of tired, but happy, walkers are often taken!

a) Write down one fact about the West Highland Way from the first paragraph.

_____

1 mark

b) Write down one opinion about the West Highland Way from the first paragraph.

_____

1 mark

c) 'The second paragraph implies that the walk is both good and bad.'

i) Is this statement true or false? _____

1 mark

ii) Give a reason for your answer.

_____

_____

_____

1 mark

d) Give two reasons why the walk is difficult, based on the information in the last two paragraphs.

_____

_____

_____

_____

2 marks

Progress Test 3

GS 4 Underline the correct word in each sentence.

a) They are **are / our** seats!

b) **Were / We're / Where** going to Florida for our holidays.

c) There was a **sale / sail** on at the clothing shop.

3 marks

S 5 In each of these sentences there is a missing silent letter. Add the missing silent letter in the space provided.

a) I was num____ from the cold.

b) The price of the concert tickets was obs___ene.

c) Blow your nose on a clean han____kerchief.

d) I bought a new garden ____nome for my back yard.

e) I heard an ec____o in the cave, when I shouted.

f) I carried my books in a ____napsack.

g) I did not want to condem____ the children, because they had tried hard.

h) Are you lis___ening?

8 marks

6 State whether each of these sentences is **fact** or **opinion**.

a) My new car is blue.

_____

b) Chocolate is the nicest food in the world!

_____

c) Nobody can speak eight different languages.

_____

d) Elephants are bigger than mice.

_____

e) Shoes always cost more than bags.

_____

5 marks

64

GPS 7 Using a thesaurus, improve the description in the passage below by changing the underlined words.

Jagram walked <u>quickly</u> towards the <u>big</u> door, because he knew that the teacher was waiting inside. He <u>walked</u> into the classroom and sat down <u>hesitantly</u> at his desk. It was his least favourite lesson, so he had brought some <u>tasty</u> sweets to pass the time. <u>Quietly</u>, he took one out of his pocket and <u>moved</u> it towards his mouth, hoping that the teacher would not see him. Unluckily for Jagram the teacher <u>saw</u> him and told him to hand over the sweets. He took them off him <u>straight away</u>. <u>Next</u>, the teacher handed them out to everyone else in the class....

Re-write the passage with your improved word choices below:

_____

_____

_____

_____

_____

_____

_____

_____

_____

_____

_____

_____

_____

_____

_____

_____

10 marks

Marks........ /40

Verbs

G Grammar   P Punctuation   S Spelling

Challenge 1

G **1** Put a tick next to the verbs that are also nouns.

a) Run ☐   d) Eat ☐

b) Throw ☐   e) Write ☐

c) Make ☐   f) Jump ☐

3 marks

Marks.......... /3

Challenge 2

G **1** Complete this table by writing the correct forms of the verb 'to play'.

	(Present Continuous Tense)	(Past Continuous Tense)
1st Person singular	I am playing	I was playing
2nd person singular		
3rd person singular		
1st person plural		
2nd person plural		
3rd person plural		

10 marks

G **2** Complete this table, again for the verb 'to play', by using all the tenses in the left-hand column.

Tense	First Person Example
Present Simple	
Present Continuous (progressive)	
Present Perfect	
Past Continuous (progressive)	
Past Perfect	
Past Perfect Continuous (progressive)	
Future	
Future Continuous (progressive)	
Future Perfect Continuous (progressive)	

9 marks

66

Marks......... /19

Verbs

Challenge 3

G **1** Change the passage below into the past tense. Use different forms of the past tense to make it make sense.

> I buy some new shoes. I pay for them with my pocket money. I take them to show my friends. My friends look at the shoes while we drink coffee in the coffee shop. We walk to the bus station.

_____

_____

_____

_____

_____

_____

_____

_____

6 marks

G **2** Read this sentence:

Chloe painted the wall.

a) What is the subject of this sentence?

_____

1 mark

b) Is this sentence written in the active or passive voice?

_____

1 mark

c) Rewrite the sentence in the other voice to that used above.

_____

_____

1 mark

Marks.......... /9

Total marks .... /31   How am I doing?

67

Adverbs and Modal Verbs

| G | Grammar | P | Punctuation | S | Spelling |

Challenge 1

G **1** Underline the modal verb which makes each of these statements definite.

    a) We **might / could / will** go to the cinema.

    b) We **may / will / could** take part in the sponsored run.

    c) They **shall / might / may** win the lottery.

                                  3 marks

G **2** Underline the adverbs in these sentences.

    a) We travelled far to go on holiday.

    b) The talented choir sang confidently.

    c) He quickly cooked a tasty meal.

3 marks

Marks.......... /6

Challenge 2

GS **1** Complete the sentences with an adverb formed from the underlined adjective.

    a) She was a <u>happy</u> girl.

        She played _____.

    b) The singer had a <u>beautiful</u> voice.

        She sang _____.

    c) He was always <u>honest</u>.

        He spoke to her _____.

    d) The sun was very <u>strong</u>.

        It was shining _____.

    e) We felt <u>sad</u> at the leaving party.

        We looked at each other _____.

5 marks

G **2** Underline the adverbial in these sentences.

    a) As soon as it arrived, we ate the food.

    b) James got up early yesterday morning.

2 marks

Marks.......... /7

Adverbs and Modal Verbs

Challenge 3

GS **1** Add adverbs into the spaces in this passage.

Mary walked _____ towards the shop.

_____ it was shut, but that didn't stop Mary. She knocked

_____ on the door and shouted _____ at the

upstairs window. A window _____ opened and a head

_____ peered out.

'Who's that?' said a voice, _____.

'It's one of your customers!' replied Mary _____.
'It's past your opening time. Why aren't you open?'

There was no reply, but the window was _____ closed
and there were sounds of movement going on, before a figure
appeared at the shop door. There was the sound of clinking keys
and the lock _____ turned and the door opened.

'I'm sorry – my alarm didn't go off. Please come in.' Mary shrugged
her shoulders _____ and strode _____ into
the shop.

'What would you like?' asked the shop assistant _____.

'Have you got any chocolate biscuits?' said Mary, while fiddling
_____ in her bag for her purse.

'I'm sorry,' replied the assistant
_____. 'We're a chemist's....'

15 marks

Marks........ /15

Total marks .... /28   How am I doing?

69

Commas

G) **Grammar**   P) **Punctuation**   S) **Spelling**

Challenge 1

P) State whether the commas are used correctly in these sentences by putting a tick or cross in the box.

1   The girls ate chips, egg and beans for their tea. ☐

2   The girls ate, chips egg and beans for tea. ☐

3   'Look at this,' he remarked. ☐

3 marks

Marks.........../3

Challenge 2

P) **1**   The following sentences contain commas. Put a cross or a tick in the correct column to indicate whether they are correct or incorrect.

a)	I love playing football, it is one of my favourite activities.	☐
b)	After playing football, we intend to go home.	☐
c)	After sunbathing all morning, we walked along the beach.	☐
d)	I'll never be able to buy a pony, the prices today are mad.	☐
e)	I cannot afford a house in London, so I am moving to Hull.	☐
f)	This is a lovely photograph, you must tell me where you bought your camera.	☐
g)	The television in my room is old, but the radio is new.	☐
h)	Considering that so many people have studied English, it is surprising that so many do not know how to use commas.	☐
i)	Germany is a very interesting country, the south has some excellent vineyards.	☐

9 marks

Marks.........../9

70

Commas

Challenge 3

GP **1** Place the commas into these sentences.

a) Jessica an excellent student is also a trainee nurse.

b) Volker watched a film *Grease* last week.

c) John was shocked when he saw his former boss Eric in the shop.

d) When I saw Mr Tingle my old Chemistry teacher I immediately thought about my time at school.

e) This idea how to use commas can be a tricky concept in English.

f) There goes Scott a great footballer who also serves on the school council.

g) Tiny my oldest pet is a Yorkshire Terrier with brown and black fur.

h) Amy the girl with her hair in a bun is in my maths class.

i) This dress made of silk and cotton was given to me by my best friend.

j) My goldfish Winona has been acting strangely for a while.

10 marks

G **2** Underline the relative clause in these sentences.

a) The village was very quiet, which suited him fine.

b) She put on her hat, which was blue.

2 marks

Marks.........../12

Total marks ..../24   How am I doing?

Hyphens, Dashes and Brackets

G) Grammar   P) Punctuation   S) Spelling

Challenge 1

GP) **1** Tick the boxes to show whether the hyphens and dashes in these sentences have been used correctly. Then write whether the sentence contains **hyphens** or **dashes**.

a) Wilfred Houston-Brown was scared of nothing. ☐ _____

b) We could – if we wanted – go swimming. ☐ _____

c) The space-cadet was very brave. ☐ _____

3 marks

Marks............/3

Challenge 2

GP) **1** Put the dashes in these sentences.

a) James Smith our clever student is standing for the Youth Parliament again.

b) Will he can he win the election?

c) James Smith footballer, head boy and general brainbox is standing for the school council too.

d) Posters, marker pens, drawing pins everything is ready.

e) There was only one thing left to do build a tree!

5 marks

GP) **2** Put the hyphens in these sentences.

a) We were stuck in the hold up on the M25.

b) I like self assembly tables.

c) I also like off the peg suits.

d) He acted in self defence.

e) I like seventeenth century houses.

5 marks

Marks........../10

72

Hyphens, Dashes and Brackets

Challenge 3

GP **1** Put a tick or cross in the boxes to say whether the brackets have been used correctly or not.

a) Winston Churchill (a famous Prime Minister) was in charge of the British Parliament during World War 2. ☐

b) The BBC (British Broadcasting Corporation) is supported by people paying an annual licence. ☐

c) Sam always had good (ideas). ☐

d) (Fred) Amy's boyfriend bought the tickets to the show. ☐

e) The dog was asleep (as usual) and was rudely awoken when the alarm went off. ☐

5 marks

GP **2** Add hyphens, dashes or brackets to these sentences.

a) My mother in law is coming for dinner tomorrow.

b) The children those who are taking part in the walk will raise a lot of money for charity.

c) It's all over now just wait and see!

d) My sister is twenty three years old.

e) My friends Helen and Jo are coming on holiday with me.

5 marks

Marks........ /10

Total marks .... /23   How am I doing?

73

Semi-colons and Colons

G) Grammar   P) Punctuation   S) Spelling

Challenge 1

GP) **1** Put a tick or cross in the boxes to state whether the colons are used correctly.

a) You have only one option: leave now, while you can. ☐

b) The recipe contained fruit: biscuits and sugar. ☐

c) I can see only one thing: the football pitch. ☐

3 marks

Marks.......... /3

Challenge 2

GP) **1** Put a tick or cross in the boxes to state whether the semi-colon is used correctly in these sentences.

a) Scotland; big mountains, lochs, midges and rain. ☐

b) I dislike cheese; it tastes strange. ☐

c) I would like to visit Yorkshire; Leeds is a great city. ☐

d) I would like to visit Staffordshire; and Wiltshire! ☐

e) Taylor is a lovely girl; I will have to ask her to marry me. ☐

f) Nick plays the accordion; it earns him money. ☐

g) In the handbag were; scissors, a nail file and her credit card. ☐

h) The rain came down; soaking wet…. ☐

i) I'm not going on holiday this year; it's too expensive! ☐

9 marks

Marks.......... /9

Semi-colons and Colons

Challenge 3

GP **1** In these sentences, cross out 'and' and 'but' and replace them with semi-colons. You might need to cross out some punctuation to make way for the semi-colon.

   a) My guitar playing is excellent and I will join a group.

   b) My camera is broken, but I have another one.

   c) The market is shut and I have no food.

   d) The weather is cold and it is snowing.

   e) The fire is on, but it is not very warm.

5 marks

GP **2** Write two sentences of your own using semi-colons.

   a) _____

   _____

   b) _____

   _____

2 marks

GP **3** In these sentences, put the colon where it is needed.

   a) There are two choices at this moment in time run away or give up.

   b) This house has everything I need three bedrooms, a fitted kitchen and a loft studio.

   c) Paul wanted to know why I didn't answer his text I hadn't received it.

   d) These are my favourite foods chips, chips, chips and chips!

   e) I bought a lot of meat at the supermarket beef, turkey, chicken and lamb.

5 marks

GP **4** Write two sentences of your own using colons.

   a) _____

   _____

   b) _____

   _____

2 marks

Marks......... /14

Total marks .... /26   How am I doing?

Noun Phrases

Challenge 1

1 Draw lines to match each noun phrase to the rest of its sentence.

At weekends people enjoy	a timid black and white kitten.
He is from	going shopping.
I adopted	the older part of town.

3 marks

G 2 Underline the noun phrase in these examples.

a) They have bought a lovely new cottage.

b) My six children go to school here.

c) Those two guitars are mine.

3 marks

Marks.......... /6

Challenge 2

G 2 Look at these sentences. Fill in the table with **yes** or **no** to say whether the words in bold are the noun phrase.

Sentence	Noun phrase?
a) I won **the main prize.**	
b) **I solved** the difficult riddle.	
c) Did you enjoy **the fashion magazine?**	
d) The girl wants **to go home.**	
e) **Horses prefer** light stables.	
f) The defendant wouldn't **answer the question.**	
g) **The boy denied** taking the money.	
h) **Writing such a criticism** is unfair.	
i) I don't like **telling off my kids.**	
j) I would love to bake **a delicious cake.**	

10 marks

Marks......... /10

Noun Phrases

Challenge 3

GPS **1**   Write 10 sentences of your own and underline the noun phrase in each.

Remember that a noun phrase includes a noun – a person, place, or thing – and the modifiers that distinguish it (e.g. 'the', 'a' and any adjectives).

a) _____

b) _____

c) _____

d) _____

e) _____

f) _____

g) _____

h) _____

i) _____

j) _____

10 marks

Marks........ /10

Total marks .... /26

How am I doing?

Progress Test 4

G **1** Change these sentences from the present tense to the past simple tense.

   a) I eat food. _____

   b) I run quickly. _____

   c) I play happily. _____

3 marks

G **2** Underline the adverb in each of these sentences.

   a) Luckily Clair received a cheque for a thousand pounds.

   b) Lucie ran quickly to the door to pick up her concert tickets.

   c) Ellie's dinner was eaten greedily by the cat.

   d) Deepak's car was working fitfully.

   e) Nick's headache was getting better slowly.

5 marks

G **3** Replace the modal verb in each of these sentences with one that is definite.

> ## Example
>
> I might go swimming. → I **will** go swimming.

   a) I may take part in the sponsored swim.

   _____

   b) I could win the star prize if I buy the winning ticket.

   _____

   c) I might take a walk this afternoon.

   _____

3 marks

G **4** Read this sentence.
The boy and his sister liked Sophie, who lived next door.

   a) Underline the subject of the sentence.

   b) Circle the object of the sentence.

   c) What is the verb in the main clause of this sentence? _____

   d) What voice is this sentence written in? _____

78

e) What name is given to the word 'who' in this sentence?

_____

GPS 5 Write one or two paragraphs of your own, about a day in your life. Your writing should include the following, used correctly:

- Five past tense verbs
- Two adverbs
- Two modal verbs
- At least one comma
- A dash or brackets
- A semi-colon or colon.

_____
_____
_____
_____
_____
_____
_____
_____
_____
_____
_____
_____
_____
_____

6 You might use the writers in these lists as style models for story writing. Circle the writer in each list who did **not** write novels.

   a) Jane Austen, Charles Dickens, William Wordsworth

   b) William Shakespeare, JK Rowling, David Walliams

   c) Charlotte Brontë, Emily Brontë, John Keats

3 marks

7 Shorten each of these sentences by crossing out one or two unnecessary words.

   a) It is absolutely essential that you bring your umbrella.

   b) The actual facts speak for themselves.

   c) Make sure you do some advance planning.

   d) An anonymous stranger just spoke to me in the street.

   e) We should collaborate together on this.

   f) We could also co-operate together.

   g) I hope to entirely eliminate the ants in the cellar.

   h) I hope I don't get harmful injuries from taking part.

   i) That is a good illustrated drawing.

   j) We should postpone this until later.

10 marks

8 Read this poem and then answer the questions.

> Way down south where bananas grow,
> A grasshopper stepped on an elephant's toe.
> The elephant said, with tears in his eyes,
> 'Pick on somebody your own size!'

   a) What is the rhyme scheme of this poem? Tick the correct answer.

     ABAB ☐   AABB ☐   ABBA ☐

1 mark

   b) Explain what makes this poem amusing.

_____

_____

_____

1 mark

GPS **9** Proof-read the passage below and correct all the mistakes that you can find. Rewrite it below.

Manny peaces of pottery were made in North staffordshire, because this was the home of the pottery industry, it was started here by Josiah Wedgwood and others several centuries ago. Small villages become towns, for example Burslem and hanley. Industrial processes are used to speed up the procsess of making pottery. The local area was well-connected to the rest of the country via the growing canal netwerk. As a result of this, goods can be shipped far and wide without breaking.

10 marks

Marks........ /53

Notes

Notes